THE SACRED **SECULAR**

Also by Dottie Escobedo-Frank

ReStart Your Church

Jesus Insurgency (with Rudy Rasmus)

Igniting Worship: Advent and Christmas Sermon Seeds

Our Common Sins: Converge Bible Studies

Give It Up! A Lenten Study for Adults

THE
SACRED
SECULAR

How God Is Using the World
to Shape the Church

Dottie Escobedo-Frank
and Rob Rynders

Abingdon Press™
Nashville

THE SACRED SECULAR:
HOW GOD IS USING THE WORLD TO SHAPE THE CHURCH

Copyright © 2016 by Abingdon Press

Library of Congress Cataloging-in-Publication Data has been requested.

ISBN 978-1-5018-1044-2

Scripture quotations unless noted otherwise are from the Common English Bible. Copyright © 2011 by the Common English Bible. All rights reserved. Used by permission. www.Common EnglishBible.com.

Scripture quotations marked (NRSV) are taken from the New Revised Standard Version of the Bible, copyright 1989, Division of Christian Education of the National Council of the Churches of Christ in the United States of America. Used by permission. All rights reserved.

16 17 18 19 20 21 22 23 24 25—10 9 8 7 6 5 4 3 2 1

MANUFACTURED IN THE UNITED STATES OF AMERICA

CONTENTS

vii

First Thoughts (Dottie)

1

Introduction: New Urbanism and the Church (Rob)

15

Chapter 1: Transcendence at 105 Degrees Fahrenheit (Dottie)

31

Chapter 2: Potlucks Are Cool Again (Rob)

45

Chapter 3: TED Is My Favorite Preacher (Dottie)

61

Chapter 4: Finding Jesus in a Bar (Rob)

77

Chapter 5: Crowdsourcing Spirituality (Dottie)

91

Chapter 6: The Gentrified Church (Rob)

113

Conclusion (Rob & Dottie)

FIRST THOUGHTS

(Dottie)

Pastors talk. In fact we talk often. Sometimes I think the soul of a pastor just needs to talk to another pastor who understands the pressures of living the Life and who loves to throw around ideas about God and people and theology and history and art—and the best places to have a cup of java or a glass of wine. When we talk together we try to solve the world's problems, and we agonize over the church, one of our great loves.

We never feel as if we have done enough in a day, and we always hold out hope for the best outcome. We aren't stuck. Though we are tired. We get up every morning thinking that today we might make a difference. We have no lack of passion. We only lack time: time to consider all the options. And more time to talk with more pastors. And time with God. We spend a lot of time addressing our concerns to God. And we pray for miracles. We still believe in them.

The miracle we really want is for the church to be the church. We are done with doing church. We are done with Programs, and Growth Plans, and Ten Steps. And we are So Done with Building

Plans and Fund Raising. (They forgot to tell us in seminary that we'd have to learn to be a quasi-architect.) You could gag us easily if you mention those words while we are talking. We believe that, more than ever, this is the time to be church. Our heart knows that nothing matters more in this time of change than for us to listen. Because, despite all our talking, we still don't know the way forward.

But the thing about pastors is that we also know how to listen. We listen, and never tell, the secret hurts and disappointments of our congregants and our community. We are the dumping well for secret waters of shame and dashed hope. So, while we love to talk to each other about theology and church stuff, we are mostly trained in deep listening. We do that as much as we breathe.

So this book has come out of a listening place. But this time we chose to listen beyond the church. We chose to listen to the world, the culture, the neighborhood. That deep listening that comes from the ground around us and the Internet waves above us. This is where we turned our ears. And we did it because we understood that when our scriptures said, "For God so loved the world . . ." that meant the world. We have been listening, and this is what we have heard so far. There will be more listening by more pastors, which will bring about more talks around the java table. Let it be so. . . .

NEW URBANISM AND THE CHURCH

(Rob)

Connor lives in downtown Phoenix. He's in his midtwenties and grew up in the Phoenix suburbs. He moved to downtown Phoenix when he started college at Arizona State University, but his primary reason for moving there wasn't for school. It was because he wanted to live downtown. He actually picked his major based on what programs were available at ASU's relatively new (at the time) downtown Phoenix campus. His peers thought he was crazy. The downtown campus was small and was at least a thirty-minute ride on public transit or campus shuttle to go to Tempe, where ASU's largest campus is based and carries with it all the attractions and amenities of a major campus and college town. The downtown campus had repurposed some existing office buildings and built a few new ones, but there wasn't much to do there outside of going to class. And popular perception was that the surrounding downtown blocks offered nothing of value for a college student. Connor, however, had been coming to downtown for a few years already. In high school he had become fascinated with the downtown arts and music scene. He'd make his parents drive him down for punk concerts as often as they'd agree to. While most were writing off Phoenix as having one of the worst downtowns in America, Connor saw what was happening under the surface. He knew in his gut that there was deep and meaningful community happening, and he wanted to be a part of it. Years later, his gut proved right: downtown Phoenix is in the thick of a development boom and cultural renaissance.

Religiously, Connor grew up in suburban Catholic and evangelical churches. While he developed a deep personal religious faith and had a significant connection to a small group of church friends, he never felt that he fully fit in at the church. When a group from his church would serve meals to the homeless in a local park he'd feel a spiritual connection, but there was still something missing: a sense of connectedness, community, and interaction with the neighborhood. He had these feelings when he attended punk concerts, rode the light rail, shopped at the farmer's market, and walked the art spaces in downtown Phoenix, but he rarely felt those feelings at church. Whatever phenomenon was happening in the downtown culture and community made him feel like he was connected to something bigger than himself. When Connor arrived in downtown Phoenix, he remained a part of a small Bible study and still identified religiously as Christian, but he couldn't find a church downtown where he felt like he fit. At some point, he stopped looking. He told me, "Eventually I had this realization that the city was connecting me to something bigger than myself. That's the whole point, right? Why wouldn't you want to be connected to something bigger than yourself? I realize you can find community in church, but at some point I became turned off by the idea that I'd only be surrounded by religious people, many of whom were so judgmental and dogmatic. Living in the city offers everyday random encounters with a diversity of people who are also interested in being a part of something that is bigger than themselves."

I asked him, "So downtown Phoenix became your church?"

Without hesitating, he replied, "Absolutely."

I met Connor early on when I was a church planter. After spending five years as a campus minister I felt called to start a new community of faith in downtown Phoenix called City Square Church. So in July 2012 I hit the streets of downtown, along with my co-pastor, Brian. (We don't recommend walking the streets of Phoenix in July.) Within a year we'd gathered enough people to launch a worship service. We had started a church.

Not long into our first year of worship, my dad came to visit from Southern California. He stayed for the weekend, and I invited him to experience worship at the church I had just helped start. Growing up, I went to church with my family almost every Sunday. We went to Asbury United Methodist Church in Livermore, California, a suburb of San Francisco. In fact, I grew up going to the same church my dad grew up in. Going to church was not a problem for my dad. This Sunday, however, he seemed a little nervous. I didn't think anything of it, though, and after the service I asked him what he thought of the service. He said, "I was pleasantly surprised!"

"Oh, you thought it was going to be bad or boring?" I asked.

"Well, no, I just thought it was going to be more 'urban.'"

I understood what he meant. His was a similar reaction that both Brian and I had received numerous times from people who didn't quite understand what we were doing. When we told most people—typically friends, family, and colleagues who lived in the suburbs—that we were starting an "urban" church, they assumed we were starting a ministry with the homeless population or doing outreach to street gangs. We quickly became known as the guys who were starting the "street ministry."

During the three years I spent in downtown Phoenix I encountered a lot of people living in homelessness, and I spent hours volunteering with amazing ministries and nonprofits that were combating homelessness and poverty (and doing it way better than we ever could on our own). Yet this was not necessarily the target audience of the new church. Brian and I had come downtown because we sensed something new was happening. As I mentioned earlier, Arizona State University had recently moved some of its programs to a new downtown campus, and along with the addition of Phoenix's light rail system, new housing developments and businesses began to pop up. With a new influx of people came new and renewed music venues, art galleries, community festivals, restaurants, and parks. All of a sudden downtown Phoenix went from being a place most people wanted to avoid to a magnet for college students, artists, musicians, and young professionals. This wasn't just happening in Phoenix; I quickly discovered that cities were becoming the place to be, particularly for the millennial generation. And it wasn't just in the obvious cities like New York, Boston, Chicago, and San Francisco, but also in Austin, Washington DC, Oakland, and even Las Vegas.

Over the last ten years a renewal has been happening in numerous cities and urban cores throughout the United States. This renewal is being led by creatives, entrepreneurs, intellectuals, community activists, and business coalitions. In many ways the suburbs make sense. They offer large houses with cheaper prices, good schools, and shopping malls aplenty. But after the burst of the housing bubble and the subsequent global recession, cities suddenly looked more sustainable and beneficial to people's bank accounts. Denser living—walking, biking, or taking mass transit to work—was suddenly more compelling (and even necessary) than living in larger and less expensive homes in the suburbs, which requires long, grueling, and expensive commutes to work and back .

In 1961, Jane Jacobs published *The Death and Life of Great American Cities*, a book that took to task city planners, governments, and developers for destroying the fabric of great cities and urban areas. She writes,

> If it appears that the rebuilt portions of cities and the endless new developments spreading beyond the cities are reducing city and countryside alike to a monotonous, unnourishing gruel, this is not strange. It all comes first-, second-, third- or fourth-hand, out of the same intellectual dish of mush, a mush in which the qualities, necessities, advantages, and behavior of great cities

have been utterly confused with the qualities, necessities, advantages and behavior of other and more inert types of settlements.[1]

Jacobs makes the case for curbing suburban sprawl and provides the recipe for what makes cities unique, interesting, vital, and sustainable places to live and thrive. *The Death and Life of Great American Cities* is still one of the core texts for anyone interested in or passionate about the survival, revitalization, and thriving of cities. Although it was written over fifty years ago, Jacobs's book is still just as relevant today.

Millennials and empty nesters are flocking to the urban core, and the cities that are benefitting the most are the ones who follow many of Jacobs's (and others who have built on her work) thoughts, ideas, and recommendations on what makes a city great, namely high mixed-use density, walkability, great neighborhoods, and the reduction of automobiles in favor of safe, reliable public transportation. These are cities that are attracting what has become known as, for better or for worse, the "Creative Class," who can make up as much as 48 percent of the workforce in growing metro areas.[2]

The term is one coined by Richard Florida in his book *The Rise of the Creative Class—Revisited.* Florida writes,

> These people engage in complex problem solving that involves a great deal of independent judgment and requires high levels of education or human capital. In addition, all members of the Creative Class—whether they are artists or engineers, musicians

---

1. Jane Jacobs, *The Death and Life of Great American Cities* (New York: Vintage Books, 1992), 16–17.
2. Richard Florida, *The Rise of the Creative Class—Revisited* (New York: Basic Books, 2014), chapter 11.

or computer scientists, writers or entrepreneurs—share a common ethos that values creativity, individuality, difference, and merit.[3]

Florida argues that the Creative Class is the fastest-growing class of worker in the United States with over forty million in the workforce today.

This resurgence of urban growth, driven by millennials and the Creative Class, has naturally sent church planters rushing to cities to start new churches. Brian and I were certainly part of this rush, because we thought that all of these new people moving to downtown certainly meant they would be looking for a church to attend.

It's not that urban centers don't already have churches. In downtowns all over the United States, aging cathedrals and sanctuaries stand tall enough to notice, offering architectural beauty and historical significance. Yet many see declining attendance each Sunday, and many of their members commute from the suburbs, having once lived in the urban core but abandoned it years ago for lawns and bigger, cheaper housing. Many people who live downtown are happy not to be a part of anything religious. However, they pray, meditate, talk about making good moral and ethical decisions, and envision how to make our world a better place. These things are private. These things have deep meaning. These things are "spiritual." These folks are "spiritual but not religious" (SBNR).

---

3. Richard Florida, *The Rise of the Creative Class—Revisited: Revised and Expanded* (New York: Basic Books, 2014), Kindle Locations 486–89.

In 2012 the Pew Research Center released a study that sent shockwaves through American religion. Their research found that "the number of Americans who do not identify with any religion continues to grow at a rapid pace. One-fifth of the U.S. public— and a third of adults under 30—are religiously unaffiliated today, the highest percentages ever in Pew Research Center polling." The latest research has indicated that the SBNR trend has accelerated in recent years. Another Pew report, in 2015, found a dramatic drop in mainline Christianity and Catholicism, while the religiously unaffiliated category grew by almost 7 percent between 2007 and 2014.[4]

During my experience as a church planter I found that plenty of people still have personal spiritual beliefs and practices. They just don't want to deal with the baggage that comes with talking about God and religion, especially Christianity. Research indicates that people have left or avoided organized religion for a variety of reasons: it's too judgmental, abusive, hypocritical, political, discriminatory, hateful, or just plain uninteresting and boring.

Shifts in cultural practices and norms have certainly played a role in the decline of religious affiliation as well. A colleague of mine once mentioned that older generations were "religious but not spiritual" while younger generations today are "spiritual but not religious." Certainly there was a time when going to church on a Sunday morning was the socially expected thing to do. As the suburbs grew and people started to move out of the cities and into bigger houses with higher fences, churches became community

---

4. "America's Changing Religious Landscape," *Pew Research Center for Religion and Public Life*, last updated on May 12, 2015, http://www.pewforum .org/2015/05/12/americas-changing-religious-landscape/.

gathering places and social clubs. Being religious was practical and normative and not so much spiritual or mystical.

Today, churches are some of the last places many young people would voluntarily walk into. That, however, does not mean that they don't hold religious beliefs. It often just means that many have given up on trying to live out their faith through institutions they no longer see as relevant. To many in society, organized religion is just no longer practical or useful. However, there seems to be, more than ever, a deep longing to connect with something bigger than oneself on spiritual and communal levels. Is there still a chance, then, that churches could once again become that place for spiritual connection, growth, and community?

While for some urban dwellers attending church is a given, many have zero interest in being a part of organized religion. This is in part because of the previously mentioned negative associations that come with religion. However, I believe it is also because this culture of "new urbanism," along with other secular trends and practices, are more relevant, meaningful, and authentic than what many churches have to offer today. While many churches in the suburbs act as the community gathering places and social hubs of their neighborhoods, the culture created in the urban core often fulfills these needs. For some, it's community and connection without all the baggage of religion, but overall it's just a more meaningful, diverse, and interesting way for many to experience those things. Regardless of whether we agree or not with their reasoning, those who are abandoning or avoiding organized religion are making their way to the city. A 2015 study by the Public Religion Research Institute found that "the religiously unaffiliated is the top 'religious' group—or tied for the top religious group—in 10 of the major metro areas."[5] If we're looking to better understand the cosmic shifts in religion and spirituality in the United States in the twenty-first century, urban centers are key to our understanding.

People are drawn to cities right now because they are looking to escape the sameness and unsustainability of the suburbs: the six-lane mega-roads, lack of walkability, lack of culture, strip malls, mega-malls, big box stores, gated neighborhoods, and chain restaurants. Instead, they are moving to cities and finding a deep sense of community in the urban core. You need only walk into one of the amazing locally owned and managed restaurants or bars in an urban center to feel the communal vibe. The same is true for the art galleries, yoga studios, co-working spaces, independent coffee shops, mixers for professionals and entrepreneurs, and community festivals—all of which create a neighborhood and small community feel in our cities. These are the new gathering places and social spaces; these are the places offering creative transformation and hope; these are the places where many are now finding meaning and connection.

How do we begin, then, to bring the conversation and practice of religion, faith, and spirituality into the urban core? How do we bring the practices of community, culture, and placemaking in the urban core to the suburbs and beyond? First, we have to understand what not to do: we can't simply transplant what works in the suburbs and believe it is appropriate for the city. I

---

5. Joanna Piacenza and Robert P. Jones, "The Top Two Religious Groups That Dominate American Cities," *PRRI*, last updated August 3, 2015, http://www.prri.org /spotlight/the-top-two-religious-traditions-that-dominate-american-cities/.

believe that, in some sense, consciously or unconsciously, people are drawn to urban centers, in part, to escape institutionalized religion. Suburban churches, for the most part, have become "attractional" churches, meaning they depend on offering the best music, sermons, buildings, and programs to attract members. Many do really good work in the community and are very generous. However, to a generation that is abandoning suburban big box stores and restaurant chains for boutiques and independent eateries, suburban churches (especially large campus churches and megachurches) risk appearing too corporate and consumeristic.[6]

Sure, you can transplant suburban church into downtown—and many denominations and large nondenominational churches are indeed transplanting suburban models into the city. They often purchase or revitalize the buildings of failed historic churches or renovate older urban buildings, then move in with hundreds of transplanted suburban members. But how will these churches and their members interact with what is already happening in these cities? Will they contribute to and enhance what is already interesting, unique, and organic about these emerging urban centers, or will they offer a homogeneous and walled-off experience that many who have come to the city are trying to escape from? I have no doubt that whatever happens they will do good work and they will change lives in the community. However, to simply "franchise" a model of church is to miss what God is doing outside of the church. So, what do we do?

---

6. "Millennials Prefer Shopping Down the Street," *The G Brief,* January 1, 2014, http://thegbrief.com/articles/millennials-prefer-shopping-down-the-street-568.

I believe we need to recognize the value in, and learn from, the places in our culture that are living out who we believe Jesus is calling us to be as individuals and as community. I often wonder what Jesus would say better mirrors his vision for the church: a congregation that goes through the motions of practicing Holy Communion, once per month, or a group of friends and neighbors who gather together after work every week to share a meal together? Or how about a twenty-something young professional who is committed to the practice of yoga every day, while many of us repeat the Lord's Prayer each Sunday yet don't have a regular practice of prayer outside of a worship service? We've been quick to judge those who prefer to hang out at a coffee shop, go on a hike, or watch TED Talks as a replacement for the Sunday morning church experience. However, is it possible that God and community can be experienced just as deeply, and perhaps more deeply for some, through these "secular" practices?

Dottie and I believe that an alternative way we can bring religion, faith, and spirituality to the surface is to recognize the work that God is already doing in the city and in wider culture. We can create space and opportunities for open and honest conversation about our beliefs and spiritual connectedness. We can identify and name those sacred spaces that provide meaning and hope for the community. We can join together as partners in showing what it means to offer grace and love to those in need. We can celebrate and mourn together through shared practices and rituals. We can vision together and challenge each other, our leaders, and elected officials to continue to create a community that offers a future of hope for all of its people and the environment we live in.

This isn't just a dream or wishful thinking. There are new communities of faith emerging all over the country who are deeply informed by and embedded in the culture of their cities. They're going beyond megachurches, creating spaces that connect people to a deep and rich notion of faith. They're connecting people to God, to their cities, and to their neighbors in a way that doesn't damn culture but embraces what God is doing through culture. Throughout this book we'll be highlighting a number of these communities we believe are shaping the future of how we organize and "do" church in American society.

The suburbs and suburban churches certainly aren't going anywhere anytime soon. However, what is happening in the urban core is ground zero for what is expanding into wider culture. The influence of urban renewal is beginning to infiltrate and transform the burbs, partly for the practical purposes of sustainability and trends but also because people are finding that it's just a more interesting, compelling, and transformative way to live. Similarly, culture isn't going to replace institutionalized religious faith and practice for everyone. Organized religion, when healthy and life-giving still has many benefits to offer the world, but things are shifting whether we want them to or not. God is indeed doing a new thing.

If I'm being honest, by the time I set out to start a new faith community, in many ways I'd become spiritual but not religious. I realized that the vast majority of students who were a part of the ministry I led at ASU were graduating and failing to connect with a church. Some would visit a mainline church to find they were by far the youngest person in the room. Or they would visit a church with plenty of people their age only to find a theology and belief system that did not align with their own.

So where were they going to stay connected with God? Where were they going to find community? As I reflect back, I realize that these were questions I was also asking myself. The draw and the lure to downtown Phoenix was about creating a new space for new people, but it was also about finding a new way to understand and practice my own faith. I was longing for connection and meaning in my own life. I was longing to experience God in community. I wasn't going downtown to "convert" people to Jesus. I was going downtown because Jesus was converting me and reconnecting me with some of the most transformative incarnations of the church. This wasn't going to be found in a church building but at people's homes, dinner tables, parks, music venues, bars, coffee shops, and elsewhere.

As our cities continue to renew and revitalize—finding their voices—religion and spirituality are playing a role in that revitalization. New paradigms of faith, religious, and spiritual practices are adding to the fabric of the city—not through the work of one church or faith community, but through the work of many and even through individuals and groups who are nonreligious. What's happening in our cities isn't perfect, and at times it's messy, but overall it's hopeful and it's beautiful and it has much to teach the church and the world. We hope that this book will help others be a part of this new thing that God is doing.

TRANSCENDENCE AT 105 DEGREES FAHRENHEIT

(Dottie)

The Yoga Experience

I had a day off. A Sunday-Day-Off. I had intended to go to church somewhere, but my body was so very weary. So I slept in instead. At about 11 a.m., the Church Hour, I went to the outdoor mall to pick up something I needed, and I was stunned to stillness when I entered the Biltmore courtyard. What I saw was an outdoor yoga class in progress. There were about two hundred people there. They were made up of all ages and included families, children, and grandparents—an eclectic mix of humanity. They were in the lotus pose, with their legs crossed and their hands in the prayer position. From my vantage point as a pastor, it looked like they were sitting there en masse, praying. And yoga meditation is a form of prayer, so actually, in my language, I walked into a spontaneous prayer meeting. The sight stunned me. It seemed like a sacred moment that I happened to invade. Like I fell into "church" and got filled up just by the sight and sound. The immediate thought that came to my mind was "culture does church!"

I had dabbled in yoga before and loved the ability to meditate with my body and soul at the same time. I wasn't deep into the "practice," as they say. I was just dabbling, looking for a new way to bring body movement into my life and finding that yoga had a sacred component that I experienced as meditative prayer. I had also tried Bikram yoga, also known as hot yoga. The experience was more humiliating than sacred. Clutching my mat, I walked in to find a group of very fit and very young persons.

Bikram is practiced at 105 degrees, and you walk into the room under the blast of heaters and fans that blow the heat around. Late, I had sat in the back by the entrance, which was the only spot left in this sweaty mass of humanity. I got into the class quickly because the music touched a deep place in my soul, and the gentle words of the instructor were encouraging and affirming. Everything was organized and prepared in such a way that I was able to jump in and set myself free to be in that moment. And there we were, strangers working together, the experienced Bikram enthusiasts alongside myself, the novice who was more "game" than sane.

After finding out that this was my first time practicing Bikram yoga, the teacher kept checking on me. Now I know hot, but this was something else! I think I became dehydrated at about minute twenty-two in the 105-degree temperature. Suddenly I was just wiped, and the concerned teacher moved me to a place by the side door and opened the door to the outside heat of 110 degrees. There was a breeze, and believe it or not, the outside felt cooler than the inside. While I barely made it to the end, what I noticed while I was losing all my body weight in water was that there was community in the room. So many offered assistance on correcting my pose and encouraged me to rest when I started staggering. At the end, as I headed toward the exit, wading through the inch-deep body of sweat on the floor, many gave me a thumbs up or words of praise. If I didn't feel like I was about to pass out, I would have returned to join this maniacal community. They made the Dehydrated Novice feel so very welcome.

Rob and I have been talking about the state of the church and the world. We have noticed that the cultural context is "doing church" in unexpected and perhaps unnoticed ways. We think it is time for the church to sit up and take notice. Something new is happening, and we are wondering if God is in the middle of it.

The Rocks Cry Out

The Palm Sunday story might have something to say about this. Jesus goes to the Mount of Olives and gives instructions for the disciples to follow. He tells them to go into the village and take a colt and bring it. He tells them that when the owner asks what they are doing, they are just to explain that "its master needs it." I'm sure there were a few words between the disciples and the owner, but maybe this man had heard about Jesus and thought it would be a good story to tell to his grandkids someday. They brought the colt to Jesus and covered it with clothing, and they lifted Jesus onto the beautiful, young equine. Jesus rode down the Mount of Olives, and crowds of people began to follow him and worship him. They said things like "Blessings on the king who comes in the name of the Lord. Peace in heaven and glory in the highest heavens" (Luke 19:38 CEB). The crowd was so passionate in their respect that they threw their clothes on the road as a sign of kingship and honor.

But there were detractors in the mass of humanity. Some Pharisees tried their best to keep Jesus in line by saying, "Teacher, scold your disciples! Tell them to stop!" (Luke 19:39b). They were always doing that: trying to correct Jesus on his behavior and his words. So Jesus must have been used to it, even expected it.

He turned to them and said, "I tell you, if they were silent, the stones would shout!"

I've never thought that there would be a day when we would see the stones cry out, but lately, Rob and I have been wondering if the church has become so silent that some stones are crying out in some places in the world. If that is the case, there is something we need to learn from this phenomenon.

Let me contrast that picture we saw in the yoga class with a different scene: I walk into church. There is a choir in the loft, but the sound system and the acoustics of the room are so dysfunctional that the sound is eaten up by the back walls instead of being projected forward into the congregation. People are standing and singing, but their voices are muffled and quiet, and their body language looks like this is a moment of rote behavior instead of a moment of full-on praise. The liveliest part of the song is that the director is fully engaged. The congregation watches, painfully, and reads the announcements in the bulletin to pass the time. When the congregation is called on to sing, they use their small, timid voices, afraid they will actually be heard in the half-empty space. The hour of "worship" progresses slowly, deliberately, and frankly, painfully. There is not a black, brown, blonde, or red head in the pews. Only shades of white and gray (with some bottled color added). If a nonchurchgoer walked into this church setting, they might think they happened into the saddest, flattest church on earth. And they probably wouldn't be able to find a reason to return, except for the sole purpose of nostalgia for grandma and "tradition."

And juxtapose that yoga class to the "welcome" that is received in the church. As a pastor, I heard many stories of unwelcoming behavior. One woman asked me if people like her, of a certain race, would be received in this Anglo church. Another person told me the story of how the church women ran him out of the kitchen when he was trying to get a glass of water, and he asked if it was because he was new or because he was black. Another man told me that when the congregation held hands and sang at the benediction, some congregants would not touch him (though they would hold hands with others). Some told me stories of being "overly welcomed" by church members and how they felt pounced-on. And one very capable and very smart single woman told me how she attended a church and not one person spoke to her, even during the "passing of the peace." I don't make these stories up, and there are so many of them that it has become apparent that this is a pattern. The yoga class gently encouraged and welcomed me, yet somehow the church gets "welcome" all wrong or not at all. It is often reported about ourselves, by ourselves, that we are "the friendliest church around." That is our opinion of ourselves, but that is not necessarily the opinion of those who are new in our midst. Our "welcome" can be off-putting when we are too eager; or it can be nonexistent when we are concerned about control and change.

So I've been wondering about what the church is doing and why and if our existence is being questioned by culture. Especially when "welcome" is felt so deeply elsewhere. And I've been wondering: when did the church get the idea that doing worship without enthusiasm was "cool"? John Wesley wrote directions for singing, which are included in the front of *The United Methodist Hymnal*. He says,

> IV. Sing lustily and with good courage. Beware of singing as if you were half dead, or half asleep; but lift up your voice with strength. Be no more afraid of your voice now, nor more ashamed of its being heard, than when you sung the songs of Satan.[1]

And if by chance some were too enthralled with the sound of their own voice, Wesley reminds them,

> VII. Above all sing *spiritually*. Have an eye to God in every word you sing. Aim at pleasing him more than yourself, or any other creature. In order to this attend strictly to the sense of what you sing, and see that your *Heart* is not carried away with the sound, but offered to God continually; so shall your singing be such as the *Lord* will approve of here, and reward when he cometh in the clouds of heaven.[2]

---

1. *The United Methodist Hymnal* (Nashville: The United Methodist Publishing House, 1989), vii.
2. Ibid.

There are more instructions, but these two attend to the problems of being too disengaged with singing/praising in worship and the problem of being too full of yourself and your sound when you "worship." Both are problems in our churches today. Not in every church, of course, but in some churches. In many churches.

The song "Shackles (Praise You)," by Mary Mary, has lyrics that point to our need to praise.

> Take the shackles off my feet so I can dance
> I just wanna praise you. I just wanna praise you.[3]

So what does God do when the church is no longer attentive to the *worship* and the *praise?* As I read the Luke scripture, I think that God will find places and ways for the earth and its peoples to cry out in worship. And I'm thinking that we are seeing that happen. I'm thinking that today we are seeing *the stones shout out.*

We are seeing the world connect with God without the help of the church. And that hurts.

The Nature Connection

Some of this behavior of connecting with God without the help of the church is as old as nature. In fact, it *is* in nature. People for ages have been saying that they best connect with God in the experience of being outdoors and in nature. For example, hiking is a common experience of getting back to the earth, breathing clean air, and getting unplugged. In the United States the famous

---

3. Mary Mary, "Shackles (Praise You)" by Erica Atkins, Tina Atkins, and Warryn Campbell, on *Thankful*, Columbia Records, 1999.

long-distance hikes include the Appalachian Trail, the Yosemite trails, Boynton Canyon in Sedona, Old Rag in Shenandoah National Park, Havasu Canyon Trail in the Grand Canyon, and Mount Pisgah Area Trails,[4] to name a few. Hiking has become a deep-rooted part of the American context, a way to experience nature and God-in-nature. Trails dot the map of cities and rural areas alike. The activity is so prominent that this year for the first time REI, an outdoors adventure store, shut down its stores on Black Friday and encouraged everyone to get out in nature instead of shopping.[5] I suspect they made a lot of money on this venture of closing down for a day, because they tapped into the heartbeat of the cultural connection to the sacred in the outdoors.

Today we are hearing people state that they commune best with God in nature and therefore have no need of the body-church.

It is true that we can connect with the Divine when we are out in nature. When we stare at the height of a redwood tree or watch a sunset or let ourselves be covered in the darkness of the stars, our souls send out praise to the Creator. When we walk paths of nature, we get a chance to commune with the tiniest of flowers and bugs, and experience the intensity of storms and rivers. People have chosen to take long hikes, like the Appalachian Trail, that take them away from the stressors of civilization for months on end. In fact, it is oft stated that these long hikes are the way to "find oneself" after being lost in a difficult circumstance of life.

---

4. "Top 100 Trails—Best Trails in North America," Trails.com, accessed August 15, 2016, https://www.trails.com/toptrails.aspx.
5. "REI #OptOutside," YouTube, October 26, 2015, https://www.youtube.com/watch?v=FOVaEawGNMM.

I think it is possible to understand the connection of God in nature without becoming pantheistic. Nature brings us to a state of wonder, and that makes us face our Creator, and *that* facing makes us worship. So, yes, there is something in our experience of nature that brings us to a connection with God. What is missing is the connection with a group of humans who are worshipping and growing in love alongside the hiker. The awe of nature is just that: awe. It is not the fullness of the body and the bride of Christ.

So what do we do with the obvious fact that so many people prefer being in nature to being in church? Perhaps it is time for the church to go to nature with them and for us to acknowledge the power of the natural setting as locations for praise, worship, forgiveness, cleansing, and restoration.

There are a few churches experimenting with this idea. Some are worshipping at the beach, like Church on the Beach in Canada. Worship on Crystal/Bay Beach on Lake Erie is just ten miles into Canada from the United States, so people from both countries attend. This nondenominational church has grown every year. They recorded an average attendance of 57 in 2011, and of 447 in 2014. They bring in new speakers every Sunday and are in a location where people who might not normally attend church can easily join in.[6] There are other outdoor experiences of church throughout the North American context; however, there is still much room to grow into new places for invitational contexts for those who care about God but have not connected to the church.

---

6. Church on the Beach, Crystal/Bay Beach, accessed August 15, 2016, http://churchonthebeach.ca.

Coffee Shop Theology

Coffee shops are one of the new front porches of society. They are not the only "front porch," but they occupy a significant part of society's gathering space. Go to any coffee shop on Sunday morning and you will see "church" happening. Couples and groups are talking together over a special order of dark roast and a pastry. Small free book exchanges are common. Study groups, interviews for companies, and small business persons who operate without offices use coffee shops as a location for business. But on Sunday morning in particular, you will frequently see an open Bible on a table and a lively discussion around it. My husband and I experienced church-at-a-coffee-shop when we were on vacation. We settled in with our lattes and shared our earphones to tune in to a live feed of one of our favorite churches. While there, we were asked a few times what we were watching, and a quick discussion about church followed. The openness to communicate and commune in a coffee shop makes for few strangers.

What is it about coffee shops that bring about quick community? Is it the rich smell of coffee and the taste of morning delicacies? Is it the short, unguarded connections with strangers? "Short" because you usually only talk for a few minutes as people flow in and out of the shop. Is it the background music and the low rumble of conversation that makes one feel like she is in the middle of life—not an outsider? Is it the freedom to go deep with someone or to walk away at leisure? Is it the lack of schedule or prescribed set of activities? Everything is free-flowing, with an element of the comfort of home. The cost is low, and the experience is deep. This is what connects us to the experience of a coffee shop.

Steven Johnson, author of *Where Good Ideas Come From: The Natural History of Innovation*, states that good ideas are born from interactions that occur in public arenas, and reminds us that the Age of Enlightenment was born in coffee houses of that day. He calls these creative spaces "liquid networks,"[7] where different perspectives and personalities come together to create a "fluidity in the conversation"[8] and spontaneous, slow-burning idea creations are born. The coffee shop is a space where people can experience culture in a short shot of time.

Just this morning I dropped into a coffee shop to do some writing on this book. A gentleman who is there every morning greeted me and asked how I was doing. He greets everyone who walks in the door and provides a pulse-beat and people-connector for the shop. He knows all the staff by name and knows their family stories. Today, after greeting me, he asked what made me happy today. I replied, "The beautiful weather and my family." His response did not shy away from life but took us into a deeper conversation, even though it was short. He's like a social philosopher in a coffee shop. I can always count on him noticing everyone who enters, and I have come to enjoy these small talks.

Churches have grabbed on to the idea of combining coffee shops and church in a variety of ways. Hope Church in Phoenix, Arizona, is led by Pastor Paul Sorenson. His leaders began by opening an Elevate Coffee Co., and the office space for the church

---

7. "How Cafe Culture Helped Make Good Ideas Happen," NPR.org, October 17, 2010, http://www.npr.org/templates/story/story.php?storyId=130595037.

8. Ibid.

is in the coffee shop. The coffee shop is a front door, a gathering space, and a venue for idea creation. The worship service is held in a school setting, and the congregation is young, vibrant, and growing.[9]

Coffee shops have become partners with new church starts in a variety of locations and across denominations. For example, The Coffee Shop Church began as a church neared death, and the new idea was born. Pastor Josh Grimes lost all but one of his fourteen members when he proposed the idea to start this new venue for church. Avenue 209 Coffee House in Lock Haven, Pennsylvania, operates both a coffee shop and a church, and has built up its church community to include two worship services.[10] The coffee shop maintains the central focus for gathering of the community, and the worship services are for those who want to connect to God. The importance of having shared space with the town and the church is not to "be known as the 'Christian' coffee house because we figured that would only attract the Christians, and then we would go out of business."[11] Instead, they created a space that is communal in nature and has a sacred arm.

Mark Batterson, pastor of National Community Church in Washington, leads a church that began out of a coffee shop. They typically meet in movie theaters but have had worship services in the basement of the coffee shop, Ebenezer's, where fellow coffee-drinkers wander down to find out what the music is about. Bat-

9. Hope Church, Phoenix, Arizona, accessed August 15, 2016, http://hope church.me.

10. "The Coffee Shop Church," ChristianCompanies.org, July 15, 2013, http://christiancompanies.org/the-coffee-shop-church/.

11. Ibid.

terson states "Coffeehouses are postmodern wells. Let's not wait for people to come to us, let's go to them."[12]

The *New York Times* reports, according to Scott L. Thumma, a professor at the Hartford Institute for Religion Research, "That strategy, blending religion with everyday activities, disarms people put off by traditional notions of church."[13] The strategy may seem new; however, its roots are ancient. And this ancient trend is the "something deeper" that needs notice. When connection and community happen in a coffee shop environment, it is not at all "new." The beginning of the Christian church experience was based in community. The early Christians would gather together for meals, for sharing of resources, and for learning more about their faith. They shared life together in homes where deep conversations could occur and deep faith could be shared.

> The believers devoted themselves to the apostles' teaching, to the community, to their shared meals, and to their prayers. A sense of Awe came over everyone. God performed many wonders and signs through the apostles. All the believers were united and shared everything. Acts 2:42-44

This faith community was rich in their love of God and care for each other.

Contrast that to the church experience today where the congregation is upset if a worship service goes five minutes over the prescribed one-hour time block, and very few feel the need to join a small group or a special Bible study. While some in the church

---

12. Amy O'Leary, "Building Congregations Around Art Galleries and Cafes as Spirituality Wanes," *The New York Times*, December 29, 2012, http://www.nytimes.com/2012/12/30/us/new-churches-focus-on-building-a-community-life.html?_r=0.

13. Ibid.

world give much of their time and resources to make sure the church is healthy, most church attenders are focused on a short, one-hour-stop ritual of duty. While it is impossible and not recommended that we return to the early days of the church, it is apparent we have lost a sense of community. And with that loss, culture has found other spaces for connection that used to happen in the church venue.

Recently, talking to a young relative who does not attend church, I asked her if there is any part of church that she misses or sees as important. Her quick reply was that she probably misses community most of all. While she can connect with God in nature and in her own quiet moments, she feels a sense of loss of connection to a larger community outside of her work and family. We are underestimating the felt need of linking that church can bring. In this time of high online connectivity and low real-time associations, the need for relating together is greater than ever. Some of this happens in third spaces like coffee shops and sports gatherings and exercise groups. These varieties of community are not to be underestimated, and they act as a glue for a society that can be deeply fragmented. And yet, I mourn the thought that the church may have moved away from being a place of community for the world. Today we go to the world's settings to experience the community we once had in church.

Is the Bride of Christ Lonely?

Weddings are celebrations that mark a change of life. They bring together friends and family and acquaintances who are ready and willing to experience the momentary spark of love and hope. We love to go to weddings. But lately I've been wondering if the Bride of Christ, the church, is more lonely than hopeful and loving. It's not that we don't have hope, nor that we don't love, for both hope and love are central to who we are. It is just that we are dwindling in significance in society, and we are missing our most valued members: the poor, the disenfranchised, and the young. The church is no longer filled with a reflection of the fullness of society, but instead is half-filled with a small and narrow segment of society.

So I've been wondering if the church is missing herself. Missing her young, her bright ideas, her lost-who-can-be-found, her hopeless-needing-hope. Have we become like the Empty Nesters who once knew the fullness of home but now are experiencing separation anxiety as the young leave and come home only for momentary visits? Is the sound of our "Silent Night" becoming literal, echoing a whisper of hope in the world full of the cacophony of diverse shouts?

Jesus said to the Pharisees that the rocks would shout out if we didn't bring our full-on praise. Some churches are, thankfully, places of prayer and worship and praise, where people can find God in a troubled world. I am so grateful for them. And some of our churches are fading, and I am both grateful for their history and sad for their current state of affairs. It is time for us to pay attention. It is possible God is up to something we know not of, and if we stop and listen, we just might find a new way.

So, we are looking—and learning—from the places where the rocks are crying out.

Chapter 2

POTLUCKS ARE COOL AGAIN

(Rob)

I n Austin, Texas, two individuals have founded Backyard Story Night, a monthly event where people gather in someone's backyard to hear stories. An article on an Austin culture blog describes how Backyard Story Night works: "The goal is simple: gather friends—and friends of friends—in a backyard to share real, unrehearsed stories. . . . Everyone brings snacks to share with the group—a snack-luck as they call it. And everyone brings a blanket or chair. People are scattered around talking to each other and their neighbors. It's as if they're all close friends, yet most of them are complete strangers." One of the organizers remarked, "There's a real hunger for connection and community in the air. That's where storytelling fits in. It's a way to connect with complete strangers. To laugh, or cry, with our fellow human beings."[1]

---

1. Jessica Pino, "Backyard Story Night: The Hottest Trend in Austin," *The Austin Knot,* last modified May 15, 2015, http://austinot.com/backyard-story -night-austin.

To many this idea of inviting large groups of complete strangers into your backyard is refreshing. Among millennials especially, there's something life-giving about coming together to connect on basic human levels. Connecting with others and building relationships with new people is interesting, compelling, and even seems necessary to deepen and strengthen our own humanity.

Neighborhoods, despite being places dense with houses and people, are too often isolating and even divisive places. This occurs when we are incapable, it is difficult, or we are unwilling to connect with our neighbors. People don't know one another, they can't get to know one another if they don't interact with one another, and they can't interact with one another if they don't see the humanity in one another. Luke 10:25-28 tells the story of the Good Samaritan, a story that is often misunderstood but is a teaching that helps us understand not just what it looks like to be a good neighbor but who we are called to see as neighbors. The text states: "Just then a lawyer stood up to test Jesus. 'Teacher,' he said, 'what must I do to inherit eternal life?' He said to him, 'What is written in the law? What do you read there?' He answered, 'You shall love the Lord your God with all your heart, and with all your soul, and with all your strength, and with all your mind; and your neighbor as yourself.' And he said to him, 'You have given the right answer; do this, and you will live.'"

If we leave this scripture passage where it ends, which we often do, these commands from Jesus are hard enough. Perhaps we're up for the challenge of loving God with all our heart, soul, strength, and mind since God forgives easily. Loving our neighbor, though? Well, my neighbors play their music too loud, their dog barks too much, and their kids won't get off my lawn. How am I supposed to love these people who are so annoying? The passage doesn't end there, however. It's just the introduction to a much deeper challenge from Jesus. The lawyer asks Jesus "And who is my neighbor?" Jesus's answer is the parable of the good Samaritan. It's the story of a man who is robbed and beaten and left in a ditch to die by the side of the road. A priest walks by without helping the man, followed by a political leader who passes on helping the man as well. But then, a Samaritan man comes by, tends to the man's wounds, then takes him to a nearby inn and pays the innkeeper to care for the man. Jesus then asks the lawyer which was the better neighbor and he answers "the one who showed him mercy," and Jesus replies "go and do likewise."

On the surface this seems like a common sense lesson. When you see someone in need, put your smugness aside and help them. What we often overlook, however, is that the Samaritans were the hated "other" in the story. Israelites and Samaritans didn't get along. Samaritans were seen us unclean and unworthy of mingling with.[2] How then could a Samaritan be a hero of the story? The original reader of this parable would have been shocked by these scandalous words. How could a Samaritan possibly be a good neighbor to someone? Wait, is Jesus trying to tell me that not only are these people capable of being loving neighbors but that I'm supposed to be a loving neighbor to them, as well?

A few years ago, I discovered some startling facts about Arizona: Only 37 percent of Arizonans believe they are treated with

---

2. Luke Timothy Johnson, *Sacra Pagina: The Gospel of Luke* (Wilmington, DE: Michael Glazier, 2006).

respect at all times in their communities, only 25 percent believe that Arizona is a good place to meet other people, and only 12 percent of Arizonans believe that the people in their community care about one another.[3] Only 12 percent? Perhaps that's because Arizona is known as a state that "values" autonomy, gun ownership, strict immigration laws, and an overall Wild West mentality. It's hard to trust your neighbor if you're constantly suspicious of them infringing on your rights, hurting you, or stealing your property. However, these trends aren't far off from national numbers. Reports state that nationally, only about one third of Americans feel that "most people can be trusted," only 20 percent of Americans frequently spend time with their neighbors, and a third have never interacted with their neighbors.[4] All of these numbers have shown a steady decline since the 1970s.

Many have pointed to the suburbs, or at least what's known as suburban "sprawl," as a primary contributing factor to the lack of trust between neighbors. Phoenix is infamous for being the poster child for sprawl: mile after mile of cookie-cutter subdivisions with three car garages, two-thousand-square-foot-plus houses, eight-foot-high block fences, all connected by six-to-eight-lane mega streets and access from all directions by various freeways. These are neighborhoods where it's typical to come home at night, pull into your garage, close it, and avoid any interaction with your neighbors. Those high walls and desert rock landscaping also discourage natural interaction between households. How can we

3. "The Arizona We Want 2.0: The Case for Action," accessed August 1, 2016, https://issuu.com/arizonawewant/docs/cfa_az_we_want_report/16?e=4459107/1216039.

4. Joe Cortright, "City Report: Less in Common," *City Observatory*, September 6, 2015, http://cityobservatory.org/less-in-common/.

trust our neighbors if we never see them or if we interact with them only when we've reported them for a neighborhood association violation?

Certainly, this isn't the case in every suburban neighborhood. Newer developments have taken cues from urban renewal and are designing planned communities to include more opportunities for neighborhood interaction. The prime example of this, in the Phoenix metro area, is a development called Agritopia, where houses have been built with less space between them, interactive space between front yards, large front sitting porches, and lower fences to create more community interaction. It also includes a large park in the center of the community, easily accessed by residents on foot or bicycle. The community restaurants, shopping, and schools are also very walkable and bikeable. There are organized community events, community gardens, and so forth. Other planned suburban developments have tried to model this, recognizing that people are looking for more urban and sustainable features.

Today's urban cores that are so attractive to altruistic millennials seem to capture the spirit of the early church. Early Christianity provided not just community for followers of Jesus but acted as an alternative to an oppressive empire. It was at minimum a way of giving people meaning and comfort in a harsh world but almost certainly also a place of hope and survival. Christianity continued to do that throughout history, and the best of Christianity still does that today. And that's why people are drawn to it. Yet what we often hear about and experience in the world is the worst of the Christian institution. People are leaving organized religion in droves because of the judgment, hatefulness, exclusivity, and hypocrisy of too many churches and church leaders. A typical response I hear given to someone who has left a church, or to someone who says they can practice religion on their own, is "but where will you find community?"

Today, urban communities and neighborhoods can provide that community without all the baggage, while Christian communities have become social clubs or have become the types of abusive and oppressive communities that they were an alternative to during the early Christian movement. There's no clearer example of this reversal than the church potluck.

Having grown up in and being a part of The United Methodist Church all of my life, I came to see the church potluck as a sign of everything that's wrong with churches today. As I was preparing to start a new urban congregation, I would often tell folks that this new gathering would never have a potluck because potlucks are the primary cause of mainline denominational church decline. So what's the first event I go to in downtown Phoenix? A potluck in an art gallery, attended primarily by twenty- and thirty-year-olds.

Following the art gallery potluck, I couldn't help but be a little embarrassed. I'd spent so much time railing against potlucks, thinking they weren't helpful because of the terrible food and "we have them because we've always had them" mindset of hospitality committees. After sharing in this experience, however, I realized it wasn't the green bean casserole that I hated (OK, I still kind of hate it). It was the contrived sense of community that churches were creating through potlucks.

36

Many churches act as community gathering places, but they are notorious for lacking ethnic, socioeconomic, and (obviously) religious diversity.[5] They're a great way to build community and to provide support for many, but they often are unhelpful in building relationships and trust across a broad spectrum of humanity. This is especially true in churches that have entrenched themselves so deeply into "tradition" that they've forgotten why they gathered in the first place.

Although we don't know the full story, we know from Paul's letter to the church in Corinth that the community gathered regularly for meals. There was disagreement, though, over how these meals should be conducted and just who exactly was supposed to be invited. Paul writes in 1 Corinthians 11:

> Now in the following instructions I do not commend you, because when you come together it is not for the better but for the worse. For, to begin with, when you come together as a church, I hear that there are divisions among you; and to some extent I believe it. Indeed, there have to be factions among you, for only so will it become clear who among you are genuine. When you come together, it is not really to eat the Lord's supper. For when the time comes to eat, each of you goes ahead with your own supper, and one goes hungry and another becomes drunk. What! Do you not have homes to eat and drink in? Or do you show contempt for the church of God and humiliate those who have nothing? What should I say to you? Should I commend you? In this matter I do not commend you! (17-22)

The issue here was that as the different Christian households gathered together as one assembly to celebrate the Lord's Supper

5. Michael Lipka, "The most and least racially diverse U.S. religious groups," July 27, 2015, http://www.pewresearch.org/fact-tank/2015/07/27/the-most-and-least-racially-diverse-u-s-religious-groups/

together, they were still abiding by the customs of the Greco-Roman power structure. The wealthiest and most powerful members got the best seats at the table, while those with less were seated elsewhere, and it sounds like those who were getting their food first were eating it before others even got theirs. They were supposed to be bonding together over a meal as equals, modeling an alternative society.[6] Paul reminds the church of who they are supposed to be—a community that cares for one another, modeling a new power structure where everyone is seen as and treated as equals. In other words, he's reminding them of their mission to love their neighbors.

For three years, during seminary, Brandon Lazarus lived in an intentional Christian community in an urban neighborhood in Dallas, Texas. On a designated night each week, he would share a meal with his housemates, but almost always other neighbors would be present, including the homeless and persons of other faiths. Brandon shared with me that one of the frequent visitors to the house was a man named Chris. He told me, "Chris first came to us for a blanket, then for something to drink. Eventually he felt comfortable coming into the house and sharing in conversation. One evening Chris was jumped by an intoxicated homeless man. He ended up in the hospital for a few days and called me to come visit him. After a few days Chris had recovered, but because of internal bleeding and some other issues he was unable to be released unless it was into someone else's care. We talked it over at the house and agreed that Chris could come live with us for a

6. Richard A. Horsley, *Abingdon New Testament Commentaries: 1 Corinthians* (Nashville: Abingdon, 1998), 160.

while. It was then over the next couple of months of living with Chris that we learned all about his life and about the life of the homeless in East Dallas."

Reflecting on his time having Chris as a roommate, Brandon was reminded what it meant to be a good neighbor: "It was not studying scripture, theology, or sociology that taught me the most about Christian community. Chris was the one who taught me about his difficult upbringing, it was Chris that taught me what it was like to be addicted to drugs or live with paranoia on the streets. It was Chris who taught me what it was like to live among the least and the lost when we would wake up every morning at 7:00 am to pray and I began to pray 'give us today our daily bread' with a new light. I was transformed by my relationship with Chris." In a straightforward (but certainly not easy) way, this is what it looks like to go into the city and into neighborhoods, to live with and learn from our neighbors. But this is difficult and sometimes impractical work. This is work that many have been called to, but this is work that would scare many of us off. While this is a clear example of what Jesus would do, it's also a hard leap for many to make and to begin inviting homeless ex-convicts into their homes. For most of us, understanding and then living out Jesus's call to be loving neighbors literally starts next door.

Organic neighborliness is the result of conditions that are created by a great environment. The way cities and neighborhoods are designed is a primary factor in the level of neighborliness in a community. In his book Walkable City, Jeff Speck makes a strong argument that walkable cities and neighborhoods make for healthier, more sustainable, and more interesting places to live.

In the book he argues that a key concept to great neighborhoods is neighborhood structure. He writes, "Neighborhood structure refers to the presence or absence of real neighborhoods, which are technically defined as being compact, diverse, and walkable. A true neighborhood has a center and an edge, and contains a wide variety of activities in close proximity within an armature of pedestrian-friendly streets and public spaces."[7] I would also argue that great neighborhood structure also leads to greater interaction and relationship-building between neighbors.

One neighborhood that is on the rise in Phoenix, in part because it's developed a great structure, is the Coronado Neighborhood. Mike Logan grew up in Baton Rouge, Louisiana, and currently lives in Phoenix in the Coronado Neighborhood with his wife Rosalia. Mike is also a musician. Growing up in the South he gained a deep appreciation for gospel music. He learned to play guitar and has been in bands most of his adult life. A couple of years ago he co-founded an annual event in his neighborhood called the "Coronado Porch Concert Series," during which folks in the neighborhood open their front porches, backyards, and homes to a couple hundred of their neighbors. Those who open their homes up provide space for musicians to perform and often offer food and drink to guests. The idea of this event is to have a good time but also to increase a sense of community and neighborliness.

This sense of neighborliness is what convinced Mike and Rosalia to move to Coronado. They were originally looking to buy a house in another part of Phoenix when someone told them they

---

7. Jeff Speck, *Walkable City* (New York: Farrar, Straus and Giroux, 2012), 144.

should take a look at the Coronado Neighborhood. They were a little hesitant at first, since the houses were smaller, but they figured it couldn't hurt. While looking at a house they noticed a stray dog wandering down the street. Soon, a person appeared and asked if they knew who the dog belonged to. They didn't; however, Mike posted a description of the dog and their location on his Facebook profile and asked if any of his friends who were connected to the neighborhood could help find the dog's owner. Within minutes numerous people responded and the dog's owner was found. This was impressive to Mike and Rosalia, not just because of the power of social media but by how fast the residents of the neighborhood came to the aid of this lost dog. "If the neighborhood was so quick to help a pet, then we could only imagine how much these neighbors would go out of their way to help a person." A couple of months later the Logans moved into the neighborhood.

I asked Mike why he thought this particular neighborhood had a higher level of neighborly cohesion than other neighborhoods in Phoenix. Mike mentioned all the things that make for a great neighborhood structure: the walkability of the neighborhood, which includes a number of shops and restaurants throughout its fabric. However, he thinks a major factor of Coronado's sense of neighborliness has to do with the way Phoenix's urban core was originally designed (or at least how it ended up coming together).

Central Avenue is the street that runs through the heart of Phoenix. The streets that run north and south to the west of Central are numbered avenues (1st, 2nd, 3rd, etc.) and numbered streets run north and south to the east of Central. Many of the neighborhoods developed on the west side ended up being wealthier neighborhoods, with large lots and homes developed for more upper-class residents, while those neighborhoods to the east offered smaller lots and houses and were more affordable for blue-collar residents. These neighborhoods, including Coronado, offer less space between homes and open-air carports instead of garages, making random encounters with neighbors more likely and frequent. Mike also speculated that when you live in a neighborhood where people just have less, in general you depend more on coming together with your neighbors. A neighborhood gathering at someone's house for a meal—or dare I say, a potluck—wasn't just about furthering a tradition but about caring and providing for one another. It was about everyone taking what little they had and combining it to create an abundant feast.

When we make neighborhoods safe gathering places where people want to share their homes, food, music, and stories, we create transformation. It's easy to see how neighborhoods can embody "church" better and more authentically than actual churches. Neighborhoods where neighbors know one another are places where neighbors help one another and build relationships with one another. Great neighborhoods are places where stories and meals are shared. They are places that break down our attitudes of scarcity and instead remind us of the rich abundance of being together in community. Neighborhoods, with the right design and/or an intentionality of people to be neighborly, are places that help us build a deep and transformative sense of community with the people who live next door to us and across the street from us, but they also make us better neighbors with the whole of humanity. Churches can be this, as well, both embedded missionally in people's homes and neighborhoods as well as in churches that have been afraid to go beyond their parking lots. Churches must also be intentional about loving their neighbors, and that includes designing an environment—physically, theologically, spiritually, and institutionally—that breaks down barriers and builds up diverse connections and relationships. It all begins with a willingness to understand and take seriously who our neighbors are. The first step to loving our neighbor is getting to know our neighbor, and if we can't care about the well-being of the person who lives next door to us, then it will be that much harder to care for the well-being of most other human beings. However, as we'll see in a later chapter, making a neighborhood a great place to live can have unintended consequences.

TED IS MY FAVORITE PREACHER

(Dottie)

t's 5 a.m., and the alarm goes off. The preacher hits the alarm and groans. Sunday has come, ready or not. She quietly grabs her computer and Bible and stumbles out of the bedroom, hoping to not wake her sleepy husband. In the kitchen, the coffee ritual begins. Teapot of hot water. Grind the coffee beans. Pour them into the french press. Plug in the computer. Teakettle whistles. Pour over aromatic grounds and wait one minute. Press. And pour. She takes her first sip with the need of an addict. "Thank You, God, for making coffee," she whispers.

With coffee in hand, she heads to her favorite spot in the quiet living room. Suddenly it feels like the favorite part of her day. The family is asleep, and peace infuses the room as the sunrise peaks through the windows. She reads her sermon one more time, making last-minute changes, and sends a copy to her iPad. Sigh. The preacher wonders if the sermon will mean anything to anyone today. She is tired, and yet she knows she'll put on her game face and preach with everything that is left inside her, which, right now, doesn't feel like much. After all, preaching is much of how she defines her work. She loves it, and yet sometimes the never-ending "tyranny of Sunday"[1] can really ruin a weekend. Trying to be wife, mom, and pastor can wear anyone thin. She loves it. And she detests the constant drain on a life. She wishes for the thousandth time that she could have one weekend off a month.

Preaching is central to the experience of the gathered church. Every church hopes for their pastor to be a powerful preacher, a fine administrator, attentive to pastoral care, and available 24/7 for emergencies. But if you had to strip the qualities down to one main one, it would be preaching. Congregations expect their pastors to deliver a sermon that is memorable and spiritual, and that makes them want to come back next week. So, in the church world, preaching is pretty important.

But preaching has become a negative descriptor to the not-church world. Phrases like "Don't preach to me!" let's someone know that they have said too much, and probably in a bossy tone. Preaching, and preachers, have a reputation in some circles of being judgmental, moralistic, monolo-gians.[2] The culture of Americans is not so impressed with preachers today. Some of that reputation is deserved, and some of it has rubbed off from a few, very public, poor examples. Preachers, in the truest sense, are people who hold up a high value of peace, mercy, and love, along with faith in God. And yet we suffer from a tarnished reputation.

---

1. Phrase heard from Rev. Dr. Kristin Longenecker.
2. A made-up word that combines "monologues" and "theologians." Meant as a derogatory critique.

But the fact is, people are not tired of hearing some good news from someone. In fact, it is my hunch that, bored with church, they have turned to other sources for inspiration and hope.

TED Talks

TED Talks, standing for "Technology, Entertainment and Design," are talks that can be accessed for a fee in a conference setting or for free online. The company began in 1984 and has evolved to be a popular phenomenon. For example, the first TED talk to be viewed by ten million viewers is "Do Schools Kill Creativity?" by Ken Robinson.[3]

TEDx Talks are spinoffs of TED Talks that can be organized on the grassroots level. The guidelines given for speaking at TEDx Talks are:

1. "Get familiar with the form." All talks are under eighteen minutes. Less is not less.

2. "Develop an idea." Know what you are talking about.

3. "Make an outline and script."

4. "Create slides." Use images and as little text as possible.

5. "Rehearse." Practice, and time yourself.

6. "Give your talk.""

7. "Savor the glory."[4]

3. "History of TED," TED, accessed June 21, 2016, https://www.ted.com/about/our-organization/history-of-ted.

4. "TEDx Speaker Guide," TED, accessed June 21, 2016, http://storage.ted.com/tedx/manuals/tedx_speaker_guide.pdf.

TED Talks: Ideas Worth Sharing (www.ted.com) have become a common location for input on all kinds of interesting ideas, from science to art to religion. Some in the world are accessing all the moral and social development they need from this format of secular "sermons," and some are substituting faith for fabulous talks.

Short Viral Videos and Other Formats

YouTube.com is another format of short (and sometimes long) videos that tend to go viral through the quick, effective delivery method of social media. These videos show acts of kindness, happy wedding moments, cute kids and animals, medical advice, and input on almost any subject matter desired. Preachers, church services, and embarrassing church moments can all be found on youtube.com. The benefit to finding information at any time is immeasurable, and the other benefit of being able to turn it off whenever one gets bored is also an advantage. The truth is, today you can receive wisdom, motivation, and self-help on almost any topic you desire. The swath of information via video is beyond imaginable, and it is the option that many choose over church and preaching.

Another venue for receiving messages of importance is podcasts. These are digitally recorded audio segments that can be followed on the Internet. I follow Leonard Sweet's podcasts[5] because I like to hear his thoughts on God in the world. Podcasts can be followed by signing up as a follower on the webpage, and typically

5. Leonard Sweet, accessed June 21, 2016, http://leonardsweet.com/podcasts/.

an e-mail alerts you that a new podcast has arrived. Vlogs, short for *video blogs* are used often by those who do not care to read but would rather listen and see the content. For a vlog experience, check out Eric's vlog from Northaven United Methodist Church in Dallas, Texas, in the footnote below.[6] Vlogs are great ways to interact with pastors and people in between the weekly worship experiences.

Television, though seen by some as old-school, is still an avenue for interaction with the community. When any news event occurs, the television is the source that many turn to. The high-quality screens and broadcasts set a high bar for the church in a world where communication is king and queen. At a recent United Methodist LEAD Conference in Los Angeles, a panel of award-winning Hollywood writers and producers explained their work in a field that is both creative and demanding. They stated that they are under pressure to produce twenty to thirty high-quality written episodes per season.[7] Contrast this to pastors who write approximately fifty-two sermons per year, not counting funerals and marriage sermons. While pastors have high demand to produce, we typically do it alone and without technical and creative support, and sometimes it seems that we are lagging behind the communication wheel. So television has an edge, even though it is not as personal as a worship event in real time.

However, I have also been struck by the way our society stops and attends to a full worship service on television when someone

6. "Pastor Eric's Vlog," Northaven United Methodist Church, December 16, 2015, https://www.northaven.org/2015/erics-vlog-december-15-2015/.

7. "Dynamic Speakers, Hollywood Writers, and Film Screening Headline UMC LEAD 2016," PNW News Blog, November 24, 2015, http://www.pnwumc.org/news/dynamic-speakers-hollywood-writers-film-screening-headline-umc-lead-2016/.

famous dies. Think of the funeral of Whitney Houston, and the memorial service in Charleston where a shooter took out a Bible study group before ending his life. Think of the presence of Pope Francis in the United States, and how we followed his every move and heard his every word by television coverage. In some way, it feels like the whole nation stops to attend to a moment of religious connection when these events are covered from the prelude to the benediction via TV news.

In fact, if meaningful worship includes an offering as a way of giving something for the good of the world, you can see this happening in many places in the world as well. Recently I attended a musical show, and at the end, the actors and actresses held out offering bags to receive donations to the charity they introduced on stage. This happens often at concerts as well. I was on a plane lately when an announcement was made of the charity of choice, and then the flight attendants walked down the aisle with an offering basket for anyone who wanted to spontaneously donate.

Many aspects of the Sunday worship service are showing up in society in ways that are unusual but vaguely familiar.

Scripture on Preaching

So, what is a Preacher to do? And how does she or he compete with these amazing formats of good words, spoken in excellence and broadcast around the world at the click of a keyboard, and for free? What do we have that the world isn't saying or doing? How do we stand out in the light of gospel?

The Scripture that speaks to our preaching in Romans 10:14-15 says this:

> So how can they call on someone they don't have faith in? And how can they have faith in someone they haven't heard of? And how can they hear without a preacher? And how can they preach unless they are sent? As it is written, How beautiful are the feet of those who announce the good news.

These words remind us that faith comes from hearing and that hearing is centered in Christ's message. So, while it is true we can get a lot of good information and inspiration from many formats, there is something different about hearing the good news of God's love in Jesus Christ. The preacher still has a place in our society.

Tonight I sit watching the news of yet another terrorist attack, this time in Paris, France. And it stirs my soul to think that tomorrow many preachers will take their pulpits, and many people will hear their message. And I'm wondering if they have taken the time to change their prepared sermon to one that will address this atrocity of our day. Will their message change things? Will they preach comfort and world peace and justice and love that cuts through every evil?

I sometimes wonder whether preachers really understand how important their role is in society. We could, if we attend to the voice of God, lead people to places where healing comes through and covers over the ills and evils of our day. Our message, the message of Christ's love, is that powerful. If we choose to be used in that way.

But sometimes we stumble and hold back in our preaching. We are worried about yet another complaint that will come through if we bring up a political or social issue. We tend to find a way to make someone mad when we speak our prophetic voice. Some church people have told me that they want a preacher that is "not political." I challenge them with the question, "Can the word of God ever really be without politics?" Everything we do has a touchstone in society, and that makes it political. But the fact that we disagree about our politics makes it hard to preach the word that will rub someone the wrong way.

Today's preachers need to speak with deep love as they deliver God's word. And they need deep courage to say the things that change our world.

Modern-Day Preachers

Is there any learning that is needed for the church around preaching and getting the message out? I think there is.

First of all, our delivery needs to be the best we have. The "best" means we prepare our sermons well, that we preach in the style that is congruent with our personalities, and that we are passionate about the message. It would be a good thing to stop preaching about that which we have no passion. Steven Pressfield, in *The War of Art*, says we let resistance wreck our purpose:

> If you believe God (and I do) you must declare Resistance evil, for it prevents us from achieving the life God intended when He endowed each of us with our own unique genius. *Genius* is a Latin word: the Romans used it to denote an inner spirit, holy and inviolable, which watches over us, guiding us to our calling. A writer writes with his genius; an artist paints with hers; everyone who creates operates from this sacramental center. It is our

soul's seat, the vessel that holds our being-in-potential, our star's beacon and Polaris.[8]

And I would add, a preacher preaches with his or her genius.

Resistance happens when we put off preparation for preaching and allow other "urgent" things to rob us of our central gift. Pressfield states the Rule of Thumb is, "The more important a call or action to our soul's evolution, the more Resistance we will feel toward pursuing it."[9]

Preaching is different from the world's messages if we bring the hope of Christ and the love of God into the world. Do not negate the importance of your work! And remember, preachers are at our best when we are the ones who have been changed by the good news.

Some preachers are not excellent orators; however, if our words are sincere and our lives are transparent and genuine, people will hear. We can always learn to become better at speaking in public, and there are many avenues to learn. One of my favorite places for preachers to hone their speaking ability is Toastmasters. These small groups work at building confidence and teaching the speaker to think on his or her feet. They lovingly correct, encourage, and call out the best in everyone in the group. Don't be ashamed to join a group such as Toastmasters if you hear that there is room for improvement. The role you play is that important.

---

8. Steven Pressfield, *The War of Art: Break Through the Blocks and Win Your Inner Creative Battles* (New York: Black Irish Entertainment, LLC, 2002), 4.

9. Ibid., 12.

Preachers can work to make their sermons shorter in some settings. However, remembering this is a cultural context, in some places, shorter would not work. But whether short or long, preachers can be sure of their message, of the direction and flow of delivery, and of having an attention-getting opener and a meaningful closing moment, and a message that matters. Jesus used story and metaphor, and I believe that today, this is still what transforms us. Storytelling is so important as a tool that George Fox Evangelical Seminary is leading a Doctorate of Ministry track called Preaching as Story.[10]

We can practice the artistry of preaching until the crowd that hears us is anxious and excited about receiving God's word week after week. That may mean we have to let go of the things that bind us and keep us from spending time in preparation and practice. Instead, we can be constrained to guard the time we need to make the gathering of the people worth every minute.

We can also join our efforts to make our messages readily available in a time when people may choose not to be in a Sunday gathering every week. Sermons can be readily available on the web so that people can hear when they are traveling, working, or unable to attend for whatever reason. Some churches are live-streaming their weekly services and are watching their count of attendance rise in the virtual realm. Some churches are even meeting virtually. In "Second Life,"[11] an Internet meeting site, church services occur in the chapel throughout the week. People

---

10. "Preaching as Story DMin PDX Fall '15 Advance," The Seminary Blog, George Fox Evangelical Seminary, July 2015, http://www.georgefox.edu/seminary/programs/dmin/preaching-as-story/index.html.

11. Second Life, accessed August 15, 2016, http://secondlife.com/my/whatnext/basics/index.php?lang=en-US.

attend as an avatar and hear music and sermons, and engage in mission opportunities. People who attend these virtual services are those who would never choose to attend the brick-and-mortar church building. Being open to new ways of preaching and bringing faith to our culture is crucial if we want to maintain a stance of relevance. Because, the truth is, we won't be relevant if we cannot be heard.

First United Methodist, Tucson

I have the privilege to travel all around the southern part of Arizona as a District Superintendent, and I am able to hear all kinds of preaching. I am not always moved by the preaching that occurs in the places you would expect it. Often I am surprised and delighted by the powerful preaching that occurs in the smallest of places, and when I hear that, I think that there might just be hope here. The businesslike thought that pops up occasionally is "She would be great in a larger church." But when I ask these pastors if they would like a larger setting, what I often hear is that they are totally jazzed by the work they are up to in their current location, and don't feel any need or desire to move "up." Those comments and that dedication to a place and a location give me hope. These fabulous preachers see that what they do matters and that every place preaching occurs is significant.

Rev. Beth Rambikur is one of those preachers who has a definite preaching voice that is loud, clear, challenging, and significant. She is serving in a church in the university center of Tucson, and this church is one that had been on a downturn in many ways. The mostly Anglo and aging congregation was unsure how to proceed and make their place vibrant again. Beth became their new pastor, and her preaching began to quietly infiltrate the essence of who they are. She brought hope. She brought intellectual challenge. She preaches social interaction. She brings humor and humbleness that disarms those reluctant to change. The building is big, old, and in need of repair. But their beautiful old building houses classes for foreign students at the University of Arizona and the Korean United Methodist Fellowship, and they work closely with the campus ministry, the Wesley Foundation. The building is open, and an eclectic mix of people from all walks of life flow through it. The parking lot is used for university students during the week. It feels like a place that I would hope all our churches could be: a place where everyone is welcome.

The congregation is in a location that is central to ministry, and you could say it is a Location Magnet. But the need for growth and development with younger, and more diverse populations, still exists. What is amazing, and what is a great hope, is that Rev. Beth preaches in a way that brings them back week after week. She preaches from strength in weakness, from courage in fear, and from hope in hopelessness. She doesn't want to leave to go to a "bigger and better" church because she sees the potential and the promise right where she is. Beth is young in years and old in wisdom. And that combination makes the word she speaks powerful in love. Beth's preaching is changing and transforming a congregation from decline to rebirth, and it is very exciting to watch.[12] When I look at preachers like Beth, I see that there is still a place for preaching, a place where the one on one presence matters and creates a better world.

Preaching and the Arts

A powerful combination that has been forgotten in the church halls is the connection of art and preaching. This occurs when we take a preaching moment and combine it with an artist's understanding and interpretation of the message. Recently I presented a talk on respectful conversations to the district pastors and lay leaders. I wanted us to be able to engage in dissenting ideas with respect, especially around controversial social issues. The church needs to learn again how to love and talk when we disagree, and we need to set a standard that is contrary to the current "yelling from the opposite edges" and contrary to the mean-spiritedness we have seen. So I backed into the talk by bringing in an artist, Terey Summers.[13]

Terey is an actress, and she has an ability to help us connect our emotions with our spirit. So she became "Eunice," a character who is a freshman in high school and, as a nerd, is mercilessly teased by her classmates. Eunice had us in tears before she brought us to this place of remembering that we are all loved and lovable. After that, and a few words about the story of my last church feeding the homeless,[14] we talked about hot topics in small

12. First United Methodist Church Tucson, accessed June 23, 2016, http://www.firstchurchtucson.org.

13. Terey Summers, accessed June 23, 2016, http://tereysummers.com.

14. Crossroads United Methodist Church, Phoenix, Arizona, accessed August 15, 2016, http://www.crossroadsphx.com.

groups. Eunice, the character who understood what it was like to be treated poorly, helped us to talk to each other with kindness and grace.

Artists are unique souls who have the ability to create a message in a manner that is surprising and often contradictory to our expectations. It is the surprise that brings openness to hear and see and experience life in a new way. The combination of art and preaching will give even the best and worst of us preachers a better communication, a better message. Artists will incorporate aspects of the religious life that will delight you. And artists will strip away "religion" to get to the core of "spiritual." Artists disarm even the hardest hearts among us. Play with this idea and see how your sermons can be transformed by art, and even how you will be transformed by the artists' understanding of the gospel.[15]

A Confession

If I could make a confession, it would be that sometimes TED Talks are my favorite teachers. I can't say they are my favorite preachers, but I can confess that they teach me in ways that no preaching class has taught. Anything culture is listening to I want to understand and learn from. Every period in history has its teachers, and for us, TED and other highly used video sites are a great way to listen and learn in the places where culture resides and connects. If I can learn from them, perhaps I can preach a message in a manner that the world can hear. I am still a student

---

15. I wrote some sermon ideas incorporating art and creativity into the preaching moments in a book called *Sermon Seeds: 40 Creative Sermon Starters* (Nashville: Abingdon, 2009).

of the world. And I am because I want to love the world in the way God loves her. And I am a student of the church. I listen to online preachers every time I get weary and need to be "preached to." This still feeds me. We still have some learning, preaching, and growing to do: growing in our compassion for what matters to God. Preach to me still—just do it well!

FINDING JESUS
IN A BAR

(Rob)

C ome on, guys, I gotta take you to just one more place."
This is a sentence that my friend Jerry Herships uses to
keep me up really late at night. It's also become a sort of
call to worship.

I first met Jerry on a rainy night in Portland, Oregon. I was
at a conference for people thinking about starting a new church,
and Jerry was there as a presenter. I had just come back to the
hotel after having dinner with another group of colleagues when
someone grabbed me in the hotel lobby and said, "Follow me.
We're going to dinner." Before I could say I just had dinner I
was dashing through the rain into the back of a rental car. Jerry
was in the car with some other people I knew, and he introduced
himself. "Where are we going?" I asked. Jerry replied, "Woodsman's Tavern. It's supposed to be one of the best new restaurants
in the United States." After getting lost in a couple of Portland

neighborhoods we finally found the place. At the time I was more accustomed to Applebee's and Outback Steakhouse, so Woodsman was my first introduction to a "foodie" restaurant. That night I tried sweetbreads and coffee brewed tableside for the first time, all served by James, a young, long-bearded fellow in skinny jeans. If this really was one of the best restaurants in the United States, that was great, but I was clearly out of my comfort zone and context.

After the meal we went back to the hotel. It was already pretty late, so I was heading for the elevators when Jerry grabbed me and said, "Hey, man, wanna grab a quick drink? There's a great bar just a block away, and I'd love to hear more of your story." Sure, how could things go wrong with one more drink? Plus, maybe I could find some food that was a little more within my comfort zone, like a bacon cheeseburger. The next four hours turned into a tour of a handful of Portland's downtown bars. But what became special about the Portland bar tour with Jerry wasn't a chance to relive my college years but a chance to observe people building community in a way I hadn't seen before. Each place we went we struck up conversations with bartenders and other customers, often sharing and hearing stories and laughter. It wasn't the touristy or trendy bars where this happened, either. These were true "dives" or neighborhood bars. These were the places the locals hung out. I learned more about Portland in those few hours than I had in the first few full days I had been there. I got that burger too.

If you've spent more than a few moments with Jerry, you know he has this knack for pulling a seat up to a bar and immediately striking up a meaningful conversation with the bartender and anyone within a ten-foot radius. It's no wonder he's started a successful "bar" ministry in Denver, Colorado. However, he and others have redefined what we think of as bar ministry, as modern-day bars themselves have become community gathering places where people come experience community, meet their neighbors, and find meaning. After Hours Denver holds church services in a handful of bars throughout downtown Denver. Services include music, a short message, scripture reading, and time for discussion, but the "call to worship" is participants making peanut butter and jelly sandwiches and sack lunches. The next day Jerry and a group of volunteers will head down to an urban park to hand out those lunches, clothing, jackets, and sometimes sleeping bags to those who are hungry and are in need. They serve communion, as well. From his experience as a bartender, stand-up comedian, and Hollywood actor, Jerry knew that when he responded to God's call to become a pastor, his ministry would be different. He knew the importance spaces like bars had in building community, and he wanted to combine that with Jesus's call to feed the hungry and clothe the naked.

The neighborhood bar is different from the sports and chain restaurant bars of the suburbs. These bars act as gathering spaces for the community. These are more interesting and compelling places to come share a drink and even a meal with neighbors, known and unknown. Even newer "urban" bars that serve gourmet food and craft beer and have interesting interiors and patios that create a sense of space where one wants to spend hours building community with family and friends.

Steve lives with his wife and their children in the Western United States. A few years ago they founded a successful micro brewery and tasting room. Religiously, Steve mostly grew up agnostic. However, in high school he started going to a nondenominational evangelical church after a friend invited him. He became a "born again" Christian and after a time of studying abroad in college he began feeling a call or "inclination" (as he puts it) to be a pastor and church planter. He began attending Bible college and ultimately ended up with a theological degree. After graduation Steve moved his family around the United States in hopes of finding a good pastoral opportunity; however, because of the Great Recession he had difficulty finding a full-time position. Eventually Steve planted his own congregation, which only lasted a couple of years before closing. The closing of the church was painful for Steve and his family and led Steve not only out of ministry but also out of organized religion completely. So what was next? Steve had been home-brewing his own craft beer for a while, which he enjoyed, and he decided to take some brewing classes to see if he could hone his craft. It quickly became more than a hobby, which led to the opening of the brewery. I asked Steve if he felt like this was a path he was called to. He replied, "We made the life change to start a brewery. It was a business, life decision. No spiritual inclinations or 'calling'—just needed to do something else than trying to do what I have always thought was my 'calling.'" Although Steve told me that his relationship with religion is almost nonexistent, I wondered if he had made a spiritual connection to and found community within the brewery. He said he doesn't really see or experience those connections personally, but that others most certainly do, stating "The Tasting Room is a place of human connection, given beer has always been seen as a social lubricant or maybe a cohesive gel for social interaction. As in many gathering places, it's a place for people to connect as human beings, and relationships do get forged. We see people create bonds over shared affinities. With regularities and rhythms, it's easy to sense when someone is 'off' and possibly going through a life struggle—and the natural thing to do is to listen and care."

Neighborhood bars and modern breweries are what one would consider "third places." According to sociology professor Ray Oldenburg, "The third place is a generic designation for a great variety of public places that host the regular, voluntary, informal, and happily anticipated gatherings of individuals beyond the realms of home and work."[1] A key characteristic of a third place, according to Oldenburg, is that it acts as a "leveler." He writes, "A place that is a leveler is, by its nature, an inclusive place. It is accessible to the general public and does not set formal criteria of membership and exclusion. There is a tendency for individuals to select their associates, friends, and intimates from among those closest in social rank. Third places, however, serve to *expand* possibilities, whereas formal associations tend to narrow and restrict them. Third places counter the tendency to be restrictive in the enjoyment of others by being open to all and by laying emphasis on the qualities not confined to status distinctions current in the society."[2] That sounds a lot like how many would describe the

1. Ray Oldenburg, *The Great Good Place: Cafes, Coffee Shops, Bookstores, Bars, Hair Salons, and Other Hangouts at the Heart of a Community* (Boston: De Capo Press, 1999), 16.
2. Ibid., 24.

idealized notion of what church should be. It sounds a whole lot like how the Bible describes what the church should be. In Galatians chapter 3, Paul writes,

> Now before faith came, we were imprisoned and guarded under the law until faith would be revealed. Therefore the law was our disciplinarian until Christ came, so that we might be justified by faith. But now that faith has come, we are no longer subject to a disciplinarian, for in Christ Jesus you are all children of God through faith. As many of you as were baptized into Christ have clothed yourselves with Christ. There is no longer Jew or Greek, there is no longer slave or free, there is no longer male and female; for all of you are one in Christ Jesus. (NRSV)

Alcohol can be controversial in many Christian circles, including in my own denomination, where alcohol is prohibited from United Methodist–owned properties. This stems from when The Methodist Episcopal Church made its anti-alcohol stance and work known during the prohibition era through the Board of Temperance, Prohibition & Public Morals. The New Testament, however, is actually quite permissive regarding alcohol. The book Divine Vintage summarizes the early church's teaching:

> Jesus's act of turning water into wine after the wedding guests were already intoxicated clearly celebrates wine as a festive gift from God and does not make a judgment about the morality of drinking. Yet Paul suggests that "it is good not to eat meat or drink wine or do anything that makes your brother or sister stumble" (Rom. 14:21). Ephesians 5:18 takes this a step further, cautioning readers: "Do not get drunk with wine, for that is debauchery; but be filled with the Spirit." Ironically, when the first Christians gathered on the day of Pentecost, they were so "filled with the spirit that others sneered and said, 'They are filled with new wine,'" which implies that spiritual ecstasy and tipsiness may produce similar behaviors (Acts 2:13). Another

passage exhorts readers to drink wine as therapy and to purify water: "No longer drink only water, but take a little wine for your stomach's sake and your frequent ailments" (1 Tim. 5:23). The same writer suggests that deacons must not indulge in much wine (1 Tim. 3:8). A bishop must not be addicted to wine (Titus 1:7). The New Testament teaches moderation, not abstinence, and allows for the occasional excess to celebrate a great event, such as the wedding at Cana, where the best wine was served last after the wedding guests were already drunk (*methuō* in Greek).[3]

There is something very sacramental about breaking bread (or raising glasses) together as neighbors. Many churches and faith-based groups have discovered partnerships with bars through Theology Pubs and Hymn Sings. Some are even having full worship services there.

During the first year of City Square Church, one of the first events we offered to the general public was Theology Pub. The idea for Theology Pub was really the idea that led to City Square. During my last year in campus ministry at Arizona State University, I was meeting with a group of graduate students for Bible study every other week. The group wanted to get off campus, and they were hungry, and well, they were thirsty too. We ended up meeting at a popular bar/restaurant off campus where we would share a meal, share about each other's lives, and then discuss a chapter of a Christian-based book that usually included reading scripture. I can still see the look on the server's face when she asked what we were doing, as she noticed beers and Bibles strewn about the table. It was somewhere between disbelieving and being very impressed.

---

3. Joel Butler, Randall Heskett, *Divine Vintage: Following the Wine Trail from Genesis to the Modern Age* (New York: St. Martin's Press, 2012), 116–17.

As the weeks went on our little beer and Bible study group got bigger and bigger. The graduate students started inviting friends, spouses, and significant others, many of whom were not students. Many of the participants wouldn't have been caught dead telling their friends that they were attending a church function; however, there was an intrigue about sitting in a bar with a pastor, talking about spiritual matters. Suddenly hanging out in a bar discussing Jesus was cool. The "cool factor" was great, but I began catching a lot of flack for doing something to be cool or trendy, which wasn't what this was all about. I found it amazing that twenty- to thirty-year-olds were opening up about their lives, having religious discussions, and asking deep questions out in the open. It wasn't that they didn't want to talk about or explore these things; it was that this was a safer and more welcoming place than the church had ever been to them or than they had perceived it to be.

Theology Pub, then, was started off of more than a hunch that people could find spiritual community in a bar. In such an ideologically polarizing world it can be near impossible to find public spaces in which you can have rational conversation and, dare I say, disagreement with another human being. Yet, before we knew it, Theology Pub became a gathering of Christians—progressive and traditional—Buddhists, atheists, agnostics, and more. The format was simple: provide some prompts relating to recent events and topics related to religion and politics, set some ground rules that encourage listening and respect, and then let people share their thoughts, opinions, and stories. I'm not sure anyone ever dramatically changed their beliefs or opinion on a matter, but they did discover what it was like to have disagreement and find common-ality without being dehumanized or dehumanizing others.[4]

Talking about theology in a downtown bar is one thing, but what about playing and singing church music in a bar? It's said often that many popular hymn tunes originated in pubs and taverns as tunes for drinking songs. Inspired by that idea, a number of Beer & Hymns events have popped up around the country. One of the most successful is Beer & Hymns OC (Orange County), which meets monthly to do exactly what the title describes: they sing hymns and religious-themed songs while drinking beer. According to an article from the Orange County Register:

> The people who flock to the gatherings include churchgoers and the unchurched, true believers and those who simply come for a good time. All are welcome, says the invitation on the Beer and Hymns Orange County website: "Maybe you grew up in the church singing these songs," it reads. "Maybe you are over church. Maybe you currently attend. Maybe it just sounds fun. Bring a friend and join us. No preaching, no proselytizing . . . just a good old-fashioned sing-a-long." And beer. Or a mixed drink, a soda, a water. There's no cover charge, no minimum drink purchase. Buying food is optional. So far, they say, nobody has acted like a drunken fool.[5]

An organizer of one of the many Beer & Hymns gatherings, which are now held throughout the United States, shared with me that while she grew up in a more evangelical tradition her family

---

4. This isn't to say that our gatherings were perfect and free from conflict. No matter how hard you try, occasionally someone is going to get their feelings hurt or someone is going to disrespect the spirit of what you are trying to do.

5. Theresa Walker, "Beer and hymns? It's not a church, but these singalongs in O.C. mix spirituatlity and ethics," *The Orange County Register*, last updated March 10, 2015, http://www.ocregister.com/articles/hymns-653489-beer-says.html.

has become more progressive and distanced themselves from institutionalized religion. Their beer and hymns community is now what they consider their spiritual community. I asked her why she thinks people resonate so well with these particular types of gatherings. She responded, "I think it's resonating with people because they love these old songs and the beautiful meaning in them. Some of our attendees are regular church-goers. Some are pastors. And some are disillusioned with the church but find that this is a setting that they can handle. It's meaningful to me because corporate worship has always been my favorite way of connecting to God, and we've found a way to do that without the baggage some people have around being hurt by the church. All are welcome."

I've lost track of how many times I've heard or read the words "all are welcome at this church." Regardless of how many times they use this phrase, too many churches have become social clubs with their own hierarchy and distinctions between members, creating very unwelcoming communities of faith. I believe this is often unintentional, but that cannot stand as an excuse. Welcoming and safe should be the default of Christian community; however, by institutionalizing something with a building, norms, leadership, and customs, it's near impossible for an established church to feel unpretentious to outsiders, regardless of how welcoming it believes itself to be. Though this idea of church in a bar or bar as church is scandalous for some, it's not a stretch for many to feel more welcome and safe in a neighborhood pub, at a craft brewery, talking about theology, or even singing hymns in a bar, than they are in a church. I don't think alcohol acts as a magic potion that makes a place more friendly and community oriented, but it's that atmosphere that breaks down walls and lets you bring your true self to the table, without fear of being judged, that makes a bar such a great gathering spot. What can churches learn from bars that would truly make them more welcoming, authentic, safe, and transformational places?

Some might say, "Sure, you can find community in a bar, and even sing hymns in a bar, but bars and business don't give back to the community or those in need like churches do." Contrary to that belief there has been a rise in nonprofit and charity bars. Oregon Public House, a nonprofit brew-pub in Portland, Oregon, is perhaps the most well known and successful. The model works like this: the pub has partnered with a number of local charities, and when customers get their bill, they have the opportunity to vote for which charity they'd like to see a portion of their tab go to. The amount of profit that the Public House has, after expenses and "contingency savings," goes to support the various nonprofits they've partnered with. Of course, the model only works if the bar generates a profit, but that hasn't been an issue for Oregon Public House—or Okra Charity Saloon, located in Houston, Texas, which operates under a similar model. Since 2013 the owners of Okra have given away over $619,000.[6] While the bar we hosted Theology Pub at didn't operate under a charity model, they were happy to agree to give away to charity a portion of anything spent by our group during any event we held there.

---

6. Okra Charity Saloon, accessed August 1, 2016, http://friedokra.org/okra -charity-saloon.

Generosity and life/world-changing impact are core values for millennials.[7] Heather Hoskins is another one of those "spiritual but not religious" millennials who strongly believes in doing good for others. Heather grew up in Arizona and never attended church until high school when she was invited to a nondenominational Christian club that met at her school. While she was curious about some of the religious elements of the group, she continued to go primarily because of the friends she had made there. She even went on a retreat with the group and, caught up in the emotion of an altar call, gave her life to Christ. When she went to college, however, she never connected to a church or Christian ministry on campus. She found friends and spiritual connectedness in other places and never felt compelled to stay connected to Christianity. A few years after college, Heather once again was invited to church by a friend. She began attending a small house church in Phoenix that she found particularly interesting because of their focus on relationships and communion. After meeting for a few years the house church disbanded, and Heather still maintained strong relationships with many of the former church members but has never felt compelled to go back to church. Instead she finds meaning, community, and spiritual connection through yoga, spin cycle, and regular gatherings with her friends. She's also very committed to giving back to the community. Twelve years ago her cousin started a fundraiser called Tour de Bar as a way to support the charitable causes she cared most about. Today,

7. Brigid Schulte, "Millennials are actually more generous than anybody realizes," *The Washington Post*, June 24, 2015, https://www.washingtonpost.com/news/wonk/wp/2015/06/24/millennials-are-actually-more-generous-than-any-body-realizes/.

Tour de Bar involves one hundred people on bikes, participating in a pub crawl in North Central Phoenix. Each participant pays a registration fee, the vast majority of which goes to support one or more charitable causes. Participants then get a wristband that gets them discounts at each bar stop, as well as the opportunity to have fun with friends, meet new people, and support a cause. A few years ago Heather's cousin decided to let Heather take full control of the event. "It's how I give back. People get to have a good time, but most importantly I'm able to raise a couple of thousand dollars to help others."

Those who don't happen to be a part of a church or organized religion want to give back and be generous, but they also want to see their generosity maximized. There's a lot of negativity around how much of each donated dollar goes toward overhead costs at a charitable organization, and churches are notorious for having a lot of overhead. However, I think most people are okay with overhead so long as they can see the impact an organization is making in the world. Changing lives, communities, and the world, often takes professional staff and physical infrastructure to facilitate and increase positive change. Does your church know the impact it's making in people's lives, in the community, and in the world? If it does, is it telling that story well? The nonprofit pubs and bars and Heather Hoskinses of the world know their mission, know their impact, and aren't afraid to tell their stories to anyone who will listen.

A few years after we met in Portland, Jerry Herships and I were in Austin, Texas, at a conference for church leaders. I was in the hotel lobby with Jerry and a number of other conference attendees, and many of us decided it was time to head to bed. But in typical Jerry fashion he implored us to head to a bar near the hotel for a nightcap. Reluctantly, we followed him over, but as we entered the bar we noticed it was empty save for a young woman putting chairs on top of tables. She gave us the "we're closed" look. Jerry worked his magic, though, and convinced her that we would be quick and that we were excellent tippers. As we pulled up to the bar, a man appeared from the back, walked to the front entrance, and locked the door. We all gave each other the same look, acknowledging that this guy was probably the owner, and he wasn't happy that we'd pushed our way in past closing time. The man began walking toward us, but instead of sharing his displeasure with us, he walked behind the bar and struck up a conversation. He asked us what we were in town for and we said "pastor's conference." "No really, what are you here for?" That's when we all pulled out our business cards to convince him of who we were. "Methodist pastors, huh? I used to attend a United Methodist Church. In fact, I was chair of our stewardship committee." All of a sudden you could hear a pin drop. He clearly wasn't messing with us, because not only did he know what stewardship was, he wasn't afraid to admit he was the chair of the committee. He then shared with us that some friends of his had convinced him a few years earlier to move from New York to open this bar in Austin. He also bravely shared with us that he was gay, but I'm sure he figured that any group of United Methodist pastors in his bar past 11 p.m. on a weeknight were probably going to be okay with that. We asked him about the church he had attended, and he said he had gone there because he had read about their pastor in the news, how he'd gone on a hunger strike to raise awareness for LGBTQ rights. He said that was a church he needed to belong to. We spent the next couple of hours, far past closing time, sharing stories—talking about church, human rights, Jesus, and God— with the bar owner.

A few days later the owner sent Jerry an e-mail to pass along to all of us. It said, "Thanks for dropping by our pub with your friends last week. It was a pleasure to meet with you and to chat with you about beers and whiskeys and God. . . . Please drop in again if your travels bring you back to Austin." I've shared this story a number of times and people usually ask me if I think the bar owner has gone back to church since his encounter with a group of clergy in his bar. I'd be lying if I said I haven't thought that myself, but then I stop myself and realize I'm fine if he hasn't. "Church" probably happens in his bar every night. It certainly did the night we walked in and pulled up a stool.

CROWDSOURCING SPIRITUALITY

(Dottie)

We are used to the church being located in a building that looks like a church and involves a gathering of people who look and act a certain way. But today's church has different forms. We don't know what to do with them, and we don't know how to count them, but they are the "church" nonetheless. If we could embrace the new thing that is popping up among us, we might be energized with hope and surprise for the future of the beloved Mother Church.

The Sandra Bland Watch

A pastor-friend, Rev. Hannah Adair Bonner, has been standing watch at the place of Sandra Bland's death for two hundred days and counting. Sandra was arrested in a violent manner for a minor traffic violation, put in jail, and reportedly died of "suicide."

77

Since Sandra Bland died close to Hannah's home in Houston, Hannah turned her outrage to activism. She planted her presence in the parking lot of the Waller County Jail and has attended to her watch since that first day. She sits watch, walking the grounds and talking to officials and visitors alike, carrying a sign that says "#What Happened to Sandy Bland?", praying for the truth to come forward. She also tweets and Facebooks her message using the hashtags #sayhername, #sandrabland, #justiceforsandrabland, #sandystillspeaks, and #whathappenedtosandrabland. The message, diligently posted on social media, has spread to news organizations, to pastors with connections, to politicians, to county officials, and to civil rights leaders. Recently it was even referenced on *The Good Wife*.[1] When Hannah had a chance meeting with Senator Bernie Sanders, she introduced him to Sandra's mother, and he has been one of those who #sayhername. People all over the country come to the place where Hannah is standing holy ground to be with her for a moment and to join the movement. They visit, share a conversation, pray, and take a personal picture with Rev. Hannah Bonner; and they leave changed. Hannah is leading a revolution of people speaking out for unfair treatment of people of color, and her stubborn resistance to "just go away" is making a difference. The world is hearing her message, and it is as if a new form of church is rising up—a church based on the value of one life and the gathering of those who give a damn.

The Sandra Bland watch makes me think about this potential new church form. What if the new church had a gathering com-

---

1. Hannah Adair Bonner's Facebook page, accessed June 23, 2016, https://www.facebook.com/hannah.a.bonner?fref=ts.

ponent that was centered on social media? What if the call to worship, instead of the ringing of the church bells, is now the social media post? What if the prayers of the people are posted in online formats for the whole world to see, not just the local church community? What if the offering and gift to God's world is no longer primarily the passing of the plate but the joining of the mission forums like TOM's Shoes, which gives away one pair of shoes for every pair that is purchased?[2] What if hearing the message happens on church websites where more people log in weekly to listen than attend the actual gathering? What if Holy Communion happens around actual dinner tables at home or in bars? What if the singing happens as frequently at Beer & Hymns events as in the church building? What if the benedictional charge to go out in the world is no longer valid because church is happening out in the world? Can we imagine that radical of a transformation, and can we live through it?

TV: Mass Funerals and Church/News Events

Pope Francis visited the United States in 2015, making stops in Washington DC, New York, and Philadelphia. It was reported that Pope Francis was moved by the devoutness of faith that he saw in the American context, and he said, "You could see the

2. TOMS, accessed June 17, 2016, http://www.toms.com/?cid=ps _usbrand&utm_source=google&utm_medium=cpc&utm_term=tom's%20 shoes&utm_campaign=US+Brand+Misspellings+-+Exact&utm _content=sD594u4Nl_dc%7Cpcrid%7C69139351855%7Cpkw%7Ctom's%20 shoes%7Cpmt%7Ce%7C.

people pray, and this struck me a lot."[3] For the short period that he was here, you could hear people everywhere talking about his presence. Thanks to television and news coverage, people were able to see him for hours, and many made it a priority to see what he was doing and saying now. We attended church for days by following in the steps of one who captured the hearts of Americans on television. Sometimes I think that we have a need to do church periodically, as in spending a week following around a holy man on television. And then we feel full until another national event happens.

What does that say about the local church? Only that there are many ways to "go to church." And that we need to be open to the new formats that are popping up and find ways we can join in with those who are "spiritual" but not sure about wanting to be "religious." The word *religion* has so much baggage today that it is hard to say it without a barrage of critique. So, what if we drop the idea of "religion" but hold on to the idea of our faith?

Jesus and the Religious Authority

Jesus didn't mince words when he spoke to the religious authorities of his day. In Matthew 23, he condemns the Pharisees and the legal experts of the law with harsh words. He calls them "blind guides" (23:16), "hypocrites" (23:23), "whitewashed tombs" (23:27), and "snakes" and "children of snakes" (23:33). He condemns them for sending money overseas without follow-

3. Ben Brumfield, "Pope Francis surprised by warmth of Americans and devoutness of the faithful," CNN, September 28, 2015, http://www.cnn.com/2015/09/28/us/pope-trip-wrap-vatican/.

ing through on raising up people who follow after the heart of God. He condemns them for requiring a tithe while forgetting the law of "justice, peace and faith" (23:23). He calls out what is wrong in the religious circles of his day.

If we were to follow in the example of Jesus, perhaps we would need to call out what is wrong in our churches and what is not working anymore. What is wrong could be things like hypocrisy, judgmental attitudes, hate-mongering of people who are not "like us," and the non-welcoming religio-political stance toward immigrants in our midst. Jesus might join the crowds of NONES or SBNR (spiritual but not religious), whose critique for the church leaves a dirty taste in their mouths. Sometimes I get it—their message—and I almost agree.

I don't fully agree, however. And that is because of hope. I have hope that God is up to something that is changing us and that change is something we cannot form or shape to our benefit. That change is God molding us into a new creation, a new church. It hurts to be shaped, and it definitely is not comfortable. But when we yield to the hands of the Creative One, then our pain of change will be worth it.

Change is something we love to fight. The first chapter of *Being Wrong*, titled "Wrongology," begins with a quote by Moliere, "It infuriates me to be wrong when I know I'm right."[4] Schulz states,

> And far from being a mark of indifference or intolerance, wrongness is a vital part of how we learn and change. Thanks to error,

---

4. Kathryn Schulz, *Being Wrong: Adventures in the Margin of Error* (New York: HarperCollins, 2010), 3.

we can revise our understanding of ourselves and amend our ideas about the world.[5]

We are in that period of the church. The time when we need to revise our traditional understanding of "church" and figure out where we need to change to meet the needs of a world that has changed drastically.

In *Switch: How to Change Things When Change Is Hard,* Heath and Heath outline how to make a switch. Some important focuses are looking for the bright places and being sure of which moves are critical. The change processes they outline are important considerations as one moves away from the well-known and well-weathered path, and chooses to forge a new way forward.[6] I recommend the whole book to you as we begin to imagine together and take steps that will transform us so that our world can once again hear the message of God's love in our own voice. It's not that we are not heard at all, but it is that our voice is growing dim, and we need to pay attention. God's hope is what keeps me going. And when I see signs of the church surviving and thriving in places other than the church, I am both bewildered and curious. When I imagine a church that has a strong component of social media and crowdsourcing, I first think of all the problems with that model. But when I quiet my critical voice down and give it the calming balm of hope, I find that I am glad to be here to witness what God is up to in this day. I have children and

---

5. Ibid., 5.

6. Chip Heath and Dan Heath, *Switch: How to Change Things When Change Is Hard* (New York: Broadway Books, 2010), 259.

grandchildren, and it matters to me that they can connect to God and God's church in their lives.

Facebook and Twitter and Instagram

Facebook is the social media venue that is much like proclamation and announcement. Twitter is the resource which can both engage quickly with short, 140-character messages, and can post links to long, involved, deep articles on anything. Instagram is a photo- and video-sharing network that connects stories in a visual form. It can be used to engage others in the stories that matter. So, my question is, how are our churches doing in telling their stories through the formats of Facebook, Twitter, and Instagram? There are other forms, and it takes work to keep up with the new developments in this web universe, but it is important that we try.

These formats provide community to people near and far. Since Facebook began, for example, I have been able to keep up with my cousins in ways that were impossible before. Social media provides both connection and distance: connection because we share the details of our lives for anyone to see, and distance because we get to choose which details are seen. In other words, we can create our virtual lives as sterile as we choose. We do this in the church as well. We present ourselves to the person sitting next to us in the pews as "Christians without problems." We "pass the peace" with familiar strangers, all while dying inside because our husband just admitted an affair last night or our teen child is dabbling in danger and drugs again. These things go on while we smile and greet each other in church, just like they go on in Facebook when (some) choose to "dress up" the reality of life. Facebook, Twitter, and Instagram are creating communities in ways that are astounding; and yet, like the church, we have to question the depth of that community development.

The new front door to any local church is the website, and I would add, the Facebook and Twitter presence also matters. People who are interested in your church may learn about you before they set foot in your presence. The question is are their learnings on these venues true to what they will encounter in the congregation? And is your presence in social media updated with your happenings in the church? For example, is your webpage still sharing the Christmas schedule and it's already Easter? To some, that may not matter, but if we hope to connect to people under forty years of age, we need to pay attention. Learning the social media world is like learning a new language. It may not be your preferred language, but if you use it enough, it will become comfortable. And if we want to learn the accent of our new language, the people we need to listen to are those who are native to the language. This is an area where the children and young adults will lead us.

Second Life

I was introduced to Second Life in the academic setting. While working on my Doctorate of Ministry, we were required to do an online class in Second Life. I was the oldest in my cohort, and the least computer savvy, so I had to get help from my younger classmates to figure out how to attend class. They set up my computer to land in the area of the chapel, where we would meet at a certain time on a certain day. Each of us chose an avatar (mine was a youngish student with brown hair and green eyes) for our presence in this virtual world, but the voices were our own, connected through the headsets we plugged in to the computer. The person who set up my computer got me close to the chapel, but not right in it. So I learned that when I entered Second Life, I automatically landed on this cliff. And all I had to do was jump off the cliff, turn left, and make my way through some heavy woods. Finally, I would come to the ocean, where I would turn right and follow the beach until I saw the chapel. I learned I had to start early to get to class, because my journey in was a little lengthy.

But it is wild, isn't it? In our class, we would show up as our chosen avatars and have a live discussion in our own voices, and we would type and talk simultaneously about topics that our professor proscribed. Sometimes I'd sit back and think, "This is unreal!" Which it really was. Both unreal and real.

That sense of "Can this really be happening?" is the feeling we bring to this new way of being church. It won't innately make sense to us. It will feel like we are traveling on ground that we've never traveled before. We will scratch our heads in confusion and keep going on because, well, we need to finish the race.

What I want you to know about virtual sites like Second Life is that people are gathering and having church services on these sites. When I discussed this at one conference recently, a woman reported that her father, a pastor, had a church service in Second Life, and he stayed closely connected with its members. He even went so far as to travel to their home cities to do weddings and baptisms. His virtual church community had a real-life component that was an extension of his online ministry. She was animated as she described this community that began as virtual and somehow became community.

I am wondering what other venues in the virtual world are out there for us to explore? Where will we find people lurking to see if we are as real as our website portrays? Are we willing to learn a new social media language in order to become a new thing in this day?

Yelp Reviews

Another website and application that is of importance is Yelp. The online site was founded in 2004 to assist people in finding businesses, restaurants, shops, and the like. You can just post the type of business you are looking for and get a list of locations nearest to you, with connections to their websites, directions to the business, and comments or reviews posted by persons who have used their products or services. Yelp reports it had 89 million unique visitors to their site in 2015.[7]

What is important for churches to understand is that when someone is looking for a church, they can ask Yelp for help, and your church, with reviews, will show up. Many times churches are not listed with Yelp, even though this service is free; or their name is listed but with no information. When I go to other cities and want to visit a church, I check Yelp and usually go to the closest

---

7. "About Us," Yelp, accessed June 17, 2016, http://www.yelp.com/about.

church with the best reviews. We used to advertise in old formats like the telephone book, but today it is sites like Yelp that will host our church's advertisement. The interesting thing about Yelp is that anyone can review, and those reviews are difficult—sometimes impossible—to remove. So our reputation in the world is out there for everyone to see. That is both wonderful and scary.

Snapchat: The Social Media Antidote

One more format is important for us to consider. And that is Snapchat. Snapchat is a venue in which one can share pictures or videos and even short messages with friends. The unique aspect about Snapchat is that your video/photo will disappear in a few seconds, so pictures are not saved and able to be accessed forever on the Internet. In Snapchat, you can also create stories, which are groups of images or videos that are able to be accessed for a twenty-four-hour period. You can look at someone's story as many times as you want in that twenty-four-hour period, but then it will disappear. The idea of Snapchat is that you can keep up with your friends without the rest of the world being able to see. When using Snapchat, most keep their friends list short and intimate. On Snapchat, you access real life in almost-real time, and then it is up to your memory to store events. On my Facebook page I have over a thousand friends, and I am not very worried about who I friend. But I Snapchat with family and a few close friends, so I think I have five friends, and I like it that way. Snapchat is where I play real life, and where I share with my close family and a very few young friends.

Snapchat feels like it is a pushback to the Internet's invasion of privacy. Some have figured out that close friends are able to access the more "real" you and that others are not. In this communication era when the whole world knows our business, people are becoming savvy enough to shut down the windows.

Crowdsourcing the Message

Sometimes we get stuck because we are uncomfortable with the form of church. But we can recall that 500 years ago, the Reformation was born when one priest posted his complaints about the church on a door, and a movement took off because the printing press helped him spread those ideas to his world. Today Rev. Martin Luther would be posting on Facebook and advertising on Yelp, with a few in-depth articles shared on Twitter. We need not be afraid, because we have been here before. It is only the format we are afraid of, not the message.

The message is the same. God loves us. God wants us to love God and love each other as we love ourselves. The message is that God, in Jesus Christ, has given us hope that we can face the evils and traumas of our day. That hope has not changed. We need to work on some critiques that our world has given us: critiques about whether or not we are really living out the central message of our faith. We all need to work on that. I believe we can become genuinely Christ-like in our congregations and in the ways we stretch out to the world's locations of church.

It is important because today we see too many school shootings and bombings in our cities, and terror and war and hunger are part of the fabric of our lives. We don't have time to squabble about the *form* of the church when we just really need to be the church. The world needs us to stand up and *be* the church again in whatever form God calls us to.

If crowdsourcing is about gathering people together, then God is the original crowdSourcer. God called for people to pro-create and to care for each other. God organized humanity in families and tribes and kinsfolk. And we began to form ourselves in towns and cities and regions and nations. God is the original Source for the crowd, and today, more than ever, the Crowd is once again seeking communion with the Source. When we feel lonely and misunderstood, we can turn to God for community and connection. When we have made a wrong turn, God directs us back. When we don't know the way forward, God beckons us to that new direction. Crowdsourcing is nothing new when you think of it. What is new is our understanding of the new form of crowdsourcing.

Crowdsourcing our spirituality, our faith, our connection to the God of Love is what will help us get the message out faster so that the next Reformation can begin. It's already happening. The question is, Will you join in?

THE GENTRIFIED CHURCH

(Rob)

Neighborhoods with walkability, public transportation, coffee shops, restaurants, parks, and interesting public spaces all make for a great place to live. These are key factors that drive growth and renewal in the urban core. For four years I lived in a part of Phoenix that was a hot spot for urban renewal. The home we bought in that neighborhood was the first home we ever owned; however, given the same circumstances at the time we purchased it, we would have difficulty affording it today. Over the course of the four years we lived there, property values skyrocketed as upper middle class families from the suburbs flocked to the urban core of the city. It's one thing, though, for a white middle class family to be priced out of being able to walk to some trendy restaurants: many would have no problem finding more than sufficient housing farther out in the suburbs. The problem lies, however, in other parts of town where families have lived for generations and live in neighborhoods that they can afford and allow them to easily access their jobs, grocery stores, doctor's offices, children's schools, and other amenities and services.

A March 2015 article in the *Los Angeles Times* shares the story of Jose and Ana Sanchez, who thirty-one years ago came to LA as refugees from El Salvador. Throughout the years they've made enough to make ends meet while raising their two children. They'd been living in Echo Park and had benefited from rent control measures, until a developer bought the house they'd been living in. The developer plans to tear down the house and replace it with five other dwellings that will sell for over six figures each. The Sanchezes are not alone in what's happened to them: "It's not just their home that they're losing, Rocio Sanchez said. Like a lot of other longtime residents, many of them Latino, they're effectively being squeezed out of Echo Park, where apartments smaller than the home they live in are going for twice what they pay, and corner bodegas give way to $5 coffee shops."[1] The Sanchezes and many of their neighbors have become the collateral damage of what is known as gentrification.

Gentrification is a term that is thrown about pretty liberally these days. But what is it, exactly? According to Benjamin Grant, an urban planner for the City of San Francisco: "Gentrification is a general term for the arrival of wealthier people in an existing urban district, a related increase in rents and property values, and changes in the district's character and culture. The term is often used negatively, suggesting the displacement of poor communi-

---

1. Steve Lopez, "After 32 Years in Echo Park, victims of displacement by gentrifi -cation," March 14, 2015, http://www.latimes.com/local/california/la-me-0315-lopez -echo-20150313-column.html.

ties by rich outsiders."[2] In other words, making cities great again doesn't always mean making them great for everyone.

Places like San Francisco, Highland Park (Los Angeles), and Brooklyn are commonly used as the poster children for gentrification. In 2015 NPR's *Wealth & Poverty from Marketplace* podcast featured a series titled York & Fig that looked at the effect of gentrification on Highland Park, a highly ethnically diverse neighborhood in Los Angeles. In recent years gentrification has taken a strong hold on Highland Park with soaring rents and property values forcing families from their homes and businesses to make way for home renovators, property flippers, and businesses that can afford higher rents and cater to the young professionals and hipsters that are flooding the neighborhood.

One episode of York & Fig profiles a bodega that for years served the needs of a diverse neighborhood, offering affordable ethnic food staples. As the neighborhood transformed, the store has changed, as well, offering less of those staples and slowly replacing them with things like gluten-free cat food and cold-brewed coffee. This family-owned business is just one of the few to survive the gentrification process as the vast majority of other family-owned businesses have been forced to relocate or close altogether.

Some trace this recent wave of gentrification back to the growth and championing of the Creative Class. Those concerned about the effects of gentrification would argue that while artists, musicians, and entrepreneurs help bring new life to cities and neighborhoods, ultimately the idea of the Creative Class has

---

2. Benjamin Grant, "Flag Wars: What Is Gentrification?," PBS, http://www.pbs.org/pov/flagwars/what-is-gentrification/.

backfired: they've brought revitalization but also gentrification, pushing existing residences—often lower-income ethnic minorities—out of their neighborhoods because of a sudden onset of a high cost of living and skyrocketing property taxes. Many now argue that not only has this culture of new urbanism brought development that prices the most vulnerable residents out of an area, but now it's also priced out the creatives who were supposed to come in and "revitalize" the city. It looks as if, ultimately, it's developers, investors, and upper-class families who have most benefited from gentrification.

The City of Oakland, California, is undergoing an urban renaissance with a lot of tech companies moving in, which has been followed by high-end condos, shopping, restaurants, bars, and coffee shops. A few years ago when everyone was celebrating this renaissance, others put their hand up and said, "Hey, wait a minute. We have a problem here." In a 2013 article for *Grist*, journalist Susie Cagle writes: "An influx of the creative class doesn't necessarily create an urban renaissance, but it doesn't need to be an urban disaster, either." She concludes: "True community revitalization for Oakland will be led by those who see the problems, who hear the gunfire, and by those who demand not only a better life for themselves, but for their neighbors, too."[3]

Churches have also played a role in gentrification, both good and bad. Denominations and church planting organizations are focusing more than ever on the urban core. Many churches are taking advantage of redeveloped urban neighborhoods, hoping to

---

3. Susie Cagle, "From the ground up: How the create class can help spark real urban revival," *Grist*, February 20, 2013, http://grist.org/cities/from-the-ground-up-how-the-creative-class-can-help-spark-real-urban-revival/.

reach millennials, the spiritual but not religious, and this Creative Class that churches have been struggling to connect with. But often, this too comes at the expense of those who were there before gentrification.

Could it be then that addressing these issues of gentrification are the key to the role churches play in urban renewal and revitalization? Churches can be a positive force and presence during this age of gentrification through creative redevelopment, rethinking how ministry models impact communities, and using their resources to help build better neighborhood networks.

For decades, after white flight to the suburbs, it wasn't uncommon to find multiple beautiful historic church properties downtown. These buildings were built to accommodate thousands of members, but as people fled to the suburbs they became empty monuments to their own success. While many of these churches closed, some remained viable by shifting their mission then to serve their urban populations, becoming outreach centers, soup kitchens, homeless shelters, and hubs for social services.

Grace Lutheran Church (ELCA) is a small but stable congregation with a sizable campus located in downtown Phoenix. In addition to providing traditional church programs (worship, Bible study, Sunday school, etc.), they also provide a number of front-line services for members of the community experiencing homelessness. For hundreds of homeless individuals, each week they offer a pancake breakfast every Sunday, a Wednesday night meal and Bible study or civil dialogue, a clothing closet, and a heat respite program during the summer (which literally saves lives during the brutal Phoenix summer by providing food, water, and shelter). They've offered these vital ministries for years, mostly without complaint from the surrounding community.

One of the initial efforts to revitalize downtown Phoenix was through big-ticket developments such as professional sports stadiums, a shopping mall, a biomedical campus, and university facilities. Under this "if you build it they will come" mentality, the city hoped that these developments would help anchor downtown Phoenix neighborhoods and spur an era of urban revitalization. In order to move forward with these projects the city bought up and cleared numerous lots throughout Phoenix's downtown neighborhoods in anticipation of building many of these structures. While some of these projects were completed fairly quickly, many took years to come to fruition, leaving entire city blocks to lay barren in the neighborhood that includes Grace Lutheran Church.

Today, however, the city's redevelopment strategy is paying dividends, and that same neighborhood is being revitalized through numerous condominium and apartment projects, and there's a new master plan for a large city park that sits to the north of Grace Lutheran Church. As the neighborhood transforms from one of empty dirt lots to one filled with the construction equipment of developers, there's been more pressure on Grace Lutheran to change or end their programs that serve those experiencing poverty and homelessness. Grace has also been approached by developers to sell or lease part of their church property. What worries them is not an influx of new people to the neighborhood but what the effect will be on those who live on the street in their neighborhood. There is a legitimate worry that those people will be displaced as the neighborhood and park are redeveloped and that developers and new residents will make efforts to remove people who are seen as undesirable. Instead of seeking relationship with people experiencing homelessness or inviting those living on the street to be part of strategizing to end homelessness, the strategy of choice is simply to move people from neighborhood to neighborhood—which is easier, at least for those who live in homes. Grace has decided, however, that they want a revitalized neighborhood that includes all of their neighbors. Sarah Stadler, the pastor at Grace Lutheran Church, shared this with me: "For us, we have come to a place of seeing that the most valuable thing we can do is simply be in relationship with people and encourage relationships between all members of our community: folks experiencing homeless, developers, city, police, etc. Obviously, what usually happens is that folks experiencing homelessness are left out entirely of relationships with people other than with other people experiencing homelessness. And what happens as a result of that (in my opinion, which is of course, flawed) is that people who live in homes/with privilege begin to see themselves as not in need. We are not in the business of helping people who need our pity. We are called by God to live in relationship with one another, to love one another in truth and action, to really know each other. And that calling is true regardless of socioeconomic class or anything else." Although they've been approached by developers, Grace has made a decision to only develop their property if it means staying true to their mission: a mission of being in relationship and building genuine community with all those who are part of the community.

One of the ways in which urban churches, like Grace, are addressing gentrification is through strategically using their property, specifically by developing and managing affordable housing. Affordable housing is key to making cities livable, diverse, and sustainable for everyone. The onus for affordable housing often falls on government to make a commitment to zoning and other policies that encourage or require a certain percentage of housing to be affordable. According to HUD: "Families who pay more than 30 percent of their income for housing are considered cost burdened and may have difficulty affording necessities such as food, clothing, transportation and medical care. An estimated 12 million renter and homeowner households now pay more than 50 percent of their annual incomes for housing. A family with one full-time worker earning the minimum wage cannot afford the local fair-market rent for a two-bedroom apartment anywhere in the United States."[4]

Native American Connections is one of the most prominent, and most successful, affordable housing organizations in Phoenix. Over the years Native American Connections has built thousands of housing units for people in need. These have included units for families and individuals who have jobs and steady income but find it financially difficult to afford living in the city center, near their jobs and public transportation, but they have also included specialized complexes, with specialized services, for those who are transitioning from living on the streets and those who are in the midst of substance abuse recovery. Affordable housing helps those in need but also adds diversity and opportunity to the fabric of neighbor-

---

4. "Affordable Housing," HUD, accessed August 1, 2016, http://portal.hud.gov /hudportal/HUD?src=/program_offices/comm_planning/affordablehousing.

hoods and cities. These aren't the "projects" either. These complexes are well designed, well located, and many times equipped with the same amenities that market rate housing complexes have. Quality-wise there are few differences between the two types of developments. Nine times out of ten if you asked someone walking by on the street if they could tell you the difference between one of Native American Connection's affordable housing complexes and a market rate complex, they probably wouldn't be able to.

City governments, however, often carry with them politics that encourage "market rate" housing and discourage affordable housing projects, particularly because of stereotypes that are associated with those who live in affordable housing (crime, addiction, poverty, etc.), not to mention affordable projects also bring with them less property and rental tax revenue for city coffers. Affordable housing projects also receive considerable pushback from residents and businesses within the proposed neighborhoods due to many of the same generalizations. Churches, though, can take on advocacy roles in their neighborhoods, encouraging cities to build more affordable housing. Churches can also go one step further by adding affordable housing to their own properties. This has been done in a number of instances and often includes new worship and program facilities for the congregation as well. For example, Gethsemane Lutheran Church, Seattle, completely reimagined their property and space, bringing fresh vitality to their congregation while also serving the needs of the most vulnerable in their city:

> The church's brick chapel, which seats about 150, is little changed. But it's now part of a larger building that includes a jewel-like sanctuary at Stewart and Ninth, fronted with long, thin, colored panels of art glass and fused glass. "When the sun

hits it, it does amazing things in here," said architect Jim Olson, of Olson Kundig Architects. He described the building as "one of the most meaningful projects I've ever worked on." Above the church's entry and office spaces are five floors of affordable housing, built in partnership with Compass Housing Alliance. The top is capped with a rooftop garden, meant to be an oasis in the urban location. The basement is home to Mary's Place, a day shelter for homeless women and children, and to the soup and movies program, which feeds and entertains up to 120 homeless people every Sunday afternoon."[5]

Projects such as these offer perhaps a second chance for historic urban churches as well as new, innovative ways of being the heart of Christ in their neighborhoods.

Taking on a major building project, of any kind, is a big deal for any organization, and they take on additional layers of complication when they involve housing. Housing projects can be risky and expensive, and they're a very long-term commitment. They don't make sense for every urban congregation but can be a win-win situation, especially when they help a congregation serve all of their neighbors. Regardless, congregations can be a voice, be a presence for, and partner with those who are being negatively affected by gentrification.

Target Audiences Vs. Partners

Church growth strategies often talk a lot about target demographics and target audiences. We wonder how we can market to

5. Katherine Long, "Gethsemane church remodel includes affordable housing," *The Seattle Times*, last updated November 5, 2012, http://www.seattletimes.com /seattle-news/gethsemane-church-remodel-includes-affordable-housing/.

and reach particular groups of people in hopes of getting them to visit, and ultimately join, our congregations. This often disconnects us from our neighbors because it treats them as commodities and marketing categories. The constant obsessing over "getting," "attracting," or "reaching" younger generations often leads us to overlook our immediate contexts. What if we shifted from marketing and transactional mindsets for the sake of institutional survival and instead focused on partnering with, collaborating with, and walking alongside our neighbors?

One of the places I frequented as a church planter was a "coworking" space in downtown Phoenix called CO+HOOTS. According to CO+HOOTS: "Coworking involves businesses and individuals working in a shared environment. The collective share the same values and interests in the collaboration and serendipity that will happen from working with talented people in the same space. These companies work independently but oftentimes collaboratively." On any given day, I could go into CO+HOOTS, not just to work, but to refine an idea or problem solve with a realtor, computer programmer, coffee shop owner, and accountant, all of whom were within a ten-foot radius of you.

The best co-working spaces are effective not because they are a free-for-all environment but because there is a lot of intentionality behind them. In fact, they are somewhat curated environments. It's not micromanagement, but it's not anything goes either. Members of co-working spaces need to be diverse and eager to collaborate. What good is a co-working space if everyone in it is a tech startup? What if someone hates having other people around while he or she is working but just wants to be a part of the space because of the inexpensive rent?

Collaborating with others in this type of environment has enormous personal and business benefits, but the concept can also be taken to a larger level that can positively impact an entire city or region. How does this co-working concept help battle gentrification? The key is in collaborating to build strong networks and bonds. In the book *Startup Communities: Building an Entrepreneurial Ecosystem in Your City*, author Brad Feld uses Boulder, Colorado, as an example of what a vibrant city overflowing with entrepreneurs and successful startups looks like. He shares what it takes to create and sustain this environment. In his book Feld shares one key aspect that I believe is extremely important for churches: it's called *network effects*. He explains how network effects help build a successful startup culture through adding more and more people to a network who are open to collaboration and sharing. He highlights research that compares California's Silicon Valley (which had a strong network effect) and Boston's tech hub, known as "Route 128" (whose companies operated more independently in silos). Both areas were considered to be a huge seedbed for technology startups back in the 1980s: "As technology quickly changed, the Silicon Valley companies were better positioned to share information, adopt new trends, leverage innovation, and nimbly respond to new conditions. Meanwhile, vertical integration and closed systems disadvantaged many Route 128 companies during periods of technological upheaval."[6] In other

---

6. Brad Feld, *Startup Communities: Building an Entrepreneurial Ecosystem in Your City* (New York: Wiley, 2012), 24.

words, the Silicon Valley companies worked as though their success depended on the success of everyone else, offering knowledge and resources "horizontally" across companies, while the Route 128 companies fended for themselves and ultimately fizzled.

In order for open-sourced initiatives to be successful they must be collaborative and they must eventually move toward accomplishing something. For example, the mission of CO+HOOTS states: "As a community of local-minded and business-focused people, we are able to collaborate on projects, share resources and generate more success to support our livelihoods. CO+HOOTS is designed to help your business thrive." They're not just about providing inexpensive desk space and organic interactions, they want their members to thrive, be successful, and build community with one another. From personal knowledge I know that the larger mission of CO+HOOTS is to also help Phoenix thrive as a city. They want to be at the forefront of an entrepreneurial revolution that makes Phoenix a world-class city. To accomplish all of that takes vision, purpose, and hard work but also a willingness to help everyone be successful.

Some newer churches and faith communities are abandoning traditional notions of church property and real estate altogether. These startups often see building church buildings as part of the problem of church decline. The wide availability of "third spaces" offers ministry startups the ability to avoid needing their own property, unless owning/leasing a building or property are in strict alignment with and in support of their mission and vision. In some cases, however, faith communities are re-thinking how we utilize physical spaces. Valley & Mountain is a newer Untied

Methodist–related faith community in the Seattle area that has embraced the co-working concept. Despite being skeptical about owning or long-term leasing a building, they've opened their own social justice–minded co-working and event space in their neighborhood called the "Collaboratory," described as an "incubator for social change." But not just anyone can utilize the space. Those using the space must have a commitment to a social justice–oriented initiative related to business, art, music, technology, etc. They must also be willing to collaborate with others utilizing the space and services Valley & Mountain provides. They hold church services in the space on Sunday mornings, and they also see it as a home base and place of empowerment for the marginalized in their community.

Too often our churches become silos, not just walling themselves off from other churches but from neighborhoods, businesses, nonprofits, community organizations, and even local government. Adopting a co-working or collaborative mindset is a way to break out of those silos and collaborate with those around us to make our communities better. Building relationships and partnerships with our neighbors helps strengthen bonds and trust in the community. It makes for more cohesive communities, enabling people to have greater influence and voice in how their neighborhoods evolve and develop.

Churches have a few choices when it comes to being a vital part of any neighborhood, whether they are urban or suburban. Every neighborhood has needs, but it is also filled with people who have talents, gifts, and skills. Churches can be an active presence and part of the community, not just carving out some space on Sunday mornings and renting some space to community groups, but instead doing the hard work that is getting to know the gifts, talents, and assets of one another and of their neighbors. Churches can work to walk alongside one another, to connect people to God in a way that is radically inclusive, compassionate, and transformative.

A few years ago Broadway United Methodist Church, an urban church located in Indianapolis, Indiana, decided they needed to be more of a positive and active presence in their neighborhood. To get started, though, they did something controversial—they killed off all their ministries to the poor. They replaced their long-running outreach ministries to the neighborhood and started to follow a community-organizing concept called Asset Based Community Development (ABCD). ABCD is a concept that we might call co-working for neighborhoods. John McKnight, the codirector of the Asset Based Community Development Institute, says that ABCD isn't about starting with needs in a community but with the skills present in a community. He writes, "Communities are built on the gifts, skills and capacities of people who also have deficits and needs. But the unique pioneer insight is that you couldn't build a community with needs. Communities are built with the gifts of its members."[7] This is a familiar concept for Christians as Paul writes in Romans 12, "For as in one body we have many members, and not all the members have the same

---

7. John McKinght, "A Basic Guide to ABCD Community Organizing," The Asset-Based Community Development Institute, accessed August 1, 2016, http://www.abcdinstitute.org/docs/A%20Basic%20Guide%20to%20ABCD%20Community%20Organizing.pdf.

function, so we, who are many, are one body in Christ, and individually we are members one of another" (NRSV).

In Indiana, the ABCD initiative began with a long process
of listening and building relationships. The pastor, Mike Mather,
hired a man named De'Amon Harges whose job it was to walk the
neighborhood around the church and listen to people's stories:
"Harges began connecting people with common interests. Within
four blocks of the church—the same area where young people had
been dying years before—Harges found 45 backyard gardeners.
He brought them together around a meal. With no agenda. The
gardeners liked it enough that they began to meet monthly. None
of them individually had seen their green thumbs as a gift. Together, they began to realize that they had something valuable. In
a neighborhood that's part of an urban food desert, they've begun
planning their own farmer's market."[8]

I believe that ABCD is one of the most important concepts
that churches can utilize to make God's kingdom more and more
present here on earth. We spend a lot of time programming and
attracting but little time listening to our neighbors. We have the
opportunity to empower people to use their God-given gifts to
build neighborhood networks where everyone can help one another. This was not a concept foreign to those in the early church.
The book of Acts tells us that the church, despite uncertainty
and persecution, maintained a bond through communal sharing:
"Awe came upon everyone, because many wonders and signs were
being done by the apostles. All who believed were together and

8. Robert King, "Death and resurrection of an urban church," *Faith & Leader-ship*, March 24, 2015, https://www.faithandleadership.com/death-and-resurrection-urban-church.

had all things in common; they would sell their possessions and goods and distribute the proceeds to all, as any had need. Day by day, as they spent much time together in the temple, they broke bread at home and ate their food with glad and generous hearts, praising God and having the goodwill of all the people. And day by day the Lord added to their number those who were being saved" (Acts 2:43-47 NRSV).

ABCD, however, doesn't have to be adopted in a literal form like Broadway UMC. We can adopt ABCD principles in how we organize our congregations. If you think about it, church committees are formed on ABCD principles, filling them with people who have gifts and skills we believe fit. Yet we've institutionalized those committees, and they often become more about gatekeeping, hoop jumping, protecting tradition, and controlling power. What if we truly focused on the gifts that people offer and gave them authentic opportunities to let those gifts shine through?

What about ABCD's role in how we learn and grow as leaders? We've become so obsessed with experts. We tell ourselves that we can't create change because we need an expert to come in and tell us how to do better worship, hire better staff, and create more effective programs. But we can't always afford experts or we know that too often they'll just be a waste of time and money because no one will listen to their expertise. Mostly we just want the expert because we're tired, we don't know what else to do, and we're desperate for answers. I know these things because I've been there before. If we took ABCD seriously, though, we could reclaim the notion that we're surrounded by experts: church members, neighbors, friends, family, colleagues, and their connections.

In 2011 I co-founded what is now known as the LEAD Conference. For years before then I had been on various planning committees for training events and conferences that brought in professional speakers to keynote and to teach and inspire participants. However, I became concerned about what happened to participants post conference. How much had they learned, and how much would apply to their particular contexts? Did they actually make any meaningful connections? I also realized that some of the best learnings and connections were happening between participants over meals, on breaks, and late at night in the hotel bar. So LEAD was started with the notion that everyone who attended was an expert. Everyone, even speakers, is considered a participant. The conference is structured around TED-style talks, crowd-sourced breakout sessions, structured networking opportunities, and extended meals to allow extra time for participants to connect.

In their book *The Abundant Community*, McKnight and Peter Block argue that ABCD is the key to true neighborhood revitalization. They point out the differences between disconnected communities that are "consumer" oriented, dependent on experts, providers, and merchants to fulfill their needs, versus communities where individuals see themselves as "citizens" who add to the overall health, well-being, and connectedness of the community. They write,

> The greatest tragedy of the consumer life is that its practitioners do not see that the local community is abundant with the relationships that are the principal resource for rescuing themselves and their families from the failure, dependency, and isolation

that are the results of a life as a consumer and client. Their ships are sinking, and they struggle to swim to safety, ignoring the life raft at their side. The way to the good life is not through consumption. It is, instead, a path that we make by walking it with those who surround us. It is the way of a competent community recognizing its abundance. We, together, become the producers of a satisfying future. We see that if we are to be citizens, together we must be the creators and producers of our future. And if we want to be the creators and producers of our future, we must become citizens, not consumers.[9]

Far too often today's church acts as a spiritual merchant, offering services and products tailored to the needs of the consumer, hungry for entertainment and self-assurance. We can shift to a citizen mentality, caring less about what others should give to us and everything we're afraid to lose, and instead care more about the well-being of those who surround us.

This is not to say that experts don't have a place but instead to point out that true transformation starts by recognizing our own gifts, skills, and resources, and especially those of the people around us. If we can't recognize our own gifts, if we can't work together, if we can't help one another, if we can't be Christ to one another, then we've failed, and we certainly won't be able to fully extend the love of Christ to the rest of the world.

C. J. Eisenbarth Hager works for Vitalyst Health Foundation, an organization in Phoenix whose mission is "to inform, connect and support efforts to improve the health of individuals and com-

---

9. John McKnight and Peter Block, *The Abundant Community: Awakening the Power of Families and Neighborhoods* (San Francisco: Berrett-Koehler Publishers, 2010), 18.

munities in Arizona." One of their primary initiatives is "working with municipal leaders to promote healthy community design." You see, C. J.'s background isn't in healthcare; she's an urban planner. Over the past few years Vitalyst has been looking at how neighborhood and urban design affect the health and quality of life of its residents. Vitalyst has been a major backer of "Reinvent Phoenix," an initiative working to improve the quality of life in a number of underserved neighborhoods connected to Phoenix's light-rail system. While many urban renewal efforts have been focused on drawing millennials and wealthy empty-nesters to downtowns, these efforts often overlook the people who are already living there. For many, living in a well-designed urban space isn't about the cool factor or being able to be in walking distance of their favorite cold-brew coffee; it's about supporting themselves and their families and thriving as human beings. C. J. deeply cares about issues of affordability and inclusiveness when it comes to housing, transportation, and urban planning in general. She sees her work as a way to combat the negative effects of gentrification.

C. J. grew up in Topeka, Kansas, and during her grade school years her family lived in the urban core. Eventually they moved to the suburbs, and when they did, C. J. felt something missing. As an adult she realized the missing piece was the feeling of the built environment and the community togetherness of the city. When she was looking at colleges, her Catholic faith compelled her to attend a Catholic school. She settled on a Jesuit school—Marquette University in Milwaukee, Wisconsin. She had been drawn to the Jesuit's focus on spirituality but also on their broad worldview and intellectual openness. While in her senior year of college, her spiritual and intellectual connection to urban planning was suddenly made clear while working on a project for a political science class. She came across the writings on Andres Duany, a prominent urban planner, and it was like someone flipped a light switch in her head. She remembers thinking, "This is my calling, this is my moment." The concepts of urbanism she had just discovered appealed to her intellectually but also spiritually and ethically. "That was the first time I had that alignment of spiritual and intellectual connection. What professional element can I find from this?"

Today, C. J. identifies as a progressive Catholic, but her family rarely goes to church and struggles with many aspects of the church. C. J. also lives in Central Phoenix, in an historic neighborhood near a light-rail station. She strongly believes that her work is helping to make the world a better place, and she wants to instill many of her values of service to others, social justice, acceptance, and inclusivity to her children; but she also wonders if the work she is doing is enough to make a difference. She sometimes thinks that maybe going back to church would help, but then her feeling of frustration over the bureaucracy and intolerance comes rushing back. When she shared this with me at the end of our conversation, I responded, "C. J., it sounds like you're living out your faith every day you go to work. Your work is your vocation, it's what God has called you to do. To me that's religious work, that's your spiritual work." By living out her calling to make our cities better, more equitable, and just for everyone, she's teaching her kids about God in ways she may never fully realize.

CONCLUSION

(Rob & Dottie)

One evening in April 2013 I (Rob) found myself standing backstage at the Scottsdale Center for the Performing Arts. In a few minutes I would be on stage giving a talk to about eight hundred people, most of whom were complete strangers and had no idea who I was. I'd preached plenty of times in worship services to hundreds and, on a few occasions, to over a thousand people. But this was different. As I paced back and forth, rehearsing my talk in my head one last time, I took a peek on stage to see how the speaker I was about to follow was doing. He seemed to be doing fine. He was wearing a tuxedo, and pictures of backyard chickens flashed on the giant screen behind him. I looked back behind me to see the guy who was going to follow my talk. He was dressed in a Ghostbusters costume complete with a proton pack. And then it hit me: what the heck did I get myself in to?

We were all speakers at an event called Ignite Phoenix. The format of the evening included eighteen speakers (chosen through an application process), each tasked with giving a five-minute talk.

Each speaker was also required to incorporate twenty slides into their presentation, arranged and timed to finish displaying at the end of five minutes. The time would start when you begin speaking, and the microphone would turn off at exactly five minutes, whether you're done or not.

I found out about Ignite a few months earlier while having coffee with a local poet and spoken word artist who had spoken at a previous Ignite event. I was telling her how living and working in the urban core had transformed me, how I'd felt like I had undergone a religious experience, and how it strengthened my relationship with my own faith tradition. As soon as I finished telling her that, her eyes lit up and she strongly encouraged me to apply to Ignite to share that story. I went home that night and applied, but then I kind of forgot about it. A few weeks later I received an e-mail that I had been selected for my talk titled "Why Being Spiritual May Be Better Than Being Religious." I wanted to share about the sacredness and the community I'd found in the city. I wanted to share the ways the secular had helped me experience my own faith in a new way but had also increased my faith in humanity. I tried to talk myself out of it for a few days but ultimately decided to take the leap. It turned out to be one of the best decisions I had ever made.

As I stood just offstage, the stage manager fitted me with a microphone, and then I waited for my cue to go onstage. When it was time I walked on stage and found my mark. I was blinded by the stage lighting, but that was good, because I couldn't see the crowd. I started talking, the timer in front of me started ticking down, and I saw my first slide appear on my monitor. There was no turning back. I had rehearsed my talk hundreds of times by now, timing it to exactly five minutes. But about one minute in, I briefly lost my place, and my heart stopped. Somehow I got back on track and four minutes later the end of my talk was greeted with a thunderous applause (or what seemed like it). I stepped off stage and half hugged/half collapsed onto the stage manager. Adrenaline was rushing through my body. I had never experienced anything like it. The talk itself had become its own deeply spiritual moment. This book has been based off the core ideas of that talk, obviously expanding and adding to those ideas, far beyond five minutes.

I used to be concerned with the question "how can we save the church from decline and irrelevance?" Then one day I realized that what we've been trying to save is just one version of how Christianity has been practiced throughout its history. We make it seem like preserving and resuscitating the North American model of church that saw so much growth in the 1950s is the only way God can work in the world. I don't take this lightly, either. I'm at least a fourth-generation Methodist, my wife is an ordained United Methodist pastor, and we're raising our children in The United Methodist Church. The UMC has served me very well. If I hadn't grown up in such a loving and caring (and, yes, suburban) UMC, I have no idea where I'd be today. As humans we tend to want to replicate the things that have worked for us in the past, and we get frustrated when others don't see the value in what we are trying to preserve. It worked for us, so why wouldn't it work for others? There's a lot of pushback within the mainline church on those who have left the church and those who don't feel the need to give the church a chance. We charge them with being lazy or flaky. We say if they only tried harder they'd see what was really awesome about our churches, or we say "just wait—things will get better." I desperately want people to experience the same depth of relationship with God and transformation I've had through church, but I've had to realize that it's going to happen in completely different ways for many. I hope we can finally understand that people who are choosing to avoid or leave the church are not broken, flaky, or lazy. Reading the Sunday paper is interesting. Hiking is interesting. A lot of things outside of the church are more interesting and compelling for a lot of people, whether we like it or not. What would it mean as the church then to stop throwing a temper tantrum over these things and instead embrace them? How would the church be radically transformed if we stopped pouting about people leaving and instead learned from and appreciated the things and places in which they've found meaning?

Part of my job as a pastor is to sit in denominational meetings, attend conferences, and read blogs and books about how to save our preferred model of church. In those spaces, church leaders talk as though folks are just waiting outside the door waiting for us to figure out a solution so they can come to our churches in overwhelming waves. The funny thing, however, is that while we've been debating and trying to just "work harder" a lot of folks seem to be doing fine without us. There's definitely some folks who are holding out hope, but for the most part people have found their happiness and spiritual connection elsewhere.

It's time for the church to give up—not on Jesus, but on holding tightly to something that is no longer central to our mission. In the introduction of *Rise of the Creative Class*, Richard Florida offers a hypothetical anecdote where a man travels from the 1950s United States to the present day. He shares that while things may look different he'd still be familiar with cars, mass transit, refrigerators, and airplanes. However, he'd be perplexed by workplaces where white men in suits have been replaced with creative, diverse workers wearing jeans and open-collared shirts. In Florida's words, "The younger ones might sport bizarre piercings and tattoos. Women and even nonwhites would be managers. Individuality and self-expression would be valued over conformity to organizational norms—and yet these people would seem strangely puritanical to this time-traveler. His ethnic jokes would fall embarrassingly flat. His smoking would get him banished to the parking lot, and his two-martini lunches would raise genuine concern. Attitudes and expressions he had never thought about would cause repeated offense. He would continually suffer the painful feeling of not knowing how to behave."[1]

If we extended this anecdote to the modern-day mainline church, however, the man would probably be very comfortable with what he found. The same church he attended in the 1950s would probably be standing, the physical buildings and property largely unchanged. The order of worship would be similar, and a similar program, education, and committee structure would still be in place. Although there would be fewer of them, many

---

1. Richard Florida, *The Rise of the Creative Class—Revisited: Revised and Expanded* (New York: Basic Books, 2014), Kindle Locations 418–22.

people in the pews would still be the same, just older. What are the implications for the church then if we take this thought experiment seriously? What are the implications that a time traveler from sixty years ago would find a radically changed society but a church largely untouched? I think this is concerning, but I don't think it means shutting the entire thing down. It means rethinking how we organize people and deploy resources for the building of God's kingdom. It means letting go of our anxiety over money and attendance, because we've turned those things into the object of our worship and we've been fed lies that it's those things that will save us from whatever it is we think we need saving from.

Throughout this book Dottie and I have lifted up examples of not just how people with no church affiliation are finding meaning and community but also examples of faith communities that have grown from where life and community are happening outside of the property lines of our church buildings and properties.

Cities are a great analogy for where the church has been, what is currently happening with the church, and what the future of the church could be if we follow God's lead. Decades ago Jane Jacobs wrote about what went wrong with cities becoming monotonous and less interesting and compelling places. The interesting places didn't make money, so they were abandoned or had to be "saved" by suburban solutions. As a nation we thought the suburbs were the solution to our problems, and now in the twenty-first century we're returning not just to cities but to the things we long for as human beings: things that are interesting, meaningful, beautiful, creative, and sustainable. All things that build community and long-lasting relationships.

While urban churches are gaining a lot of attention and investment, the suburbs aren't going anywhere, nor should they. Many suburban cities are applying urban concepts and strategies both in how they're building for the future and fixing the past. Recently, my wife, Melissa, was appointed to pastor a United Methodist Church located outside of Tucson, Arizona. For my family this meant locating from the urban core of Phoenix to the quiet suburban town of Oro Valley. It's an area surrounded by beautiful desert and mountain views, but it lacks a town center. There are some local shops and restaurants, but they are far outnumbered by chain and big box stores. However, the Town of Oro Valley has launched the "Main Streets" project in hopes of developing a central gathering place that is "a place to walk, shop, eat and play, to be with friends and family, and that reflects the unique community character."[2] Whether or not the project ever comes to fruition, town leaders recognize that they must move beyond wide roads and shopping centers that isolate people and instead create a walkable and community-driven core that brings people together. It doesn't mean turning a small town into a big city but modifying and rearranging what already exists to create a more cohesive and sustainable community.

This is a concept that Ellen Dunham-Jones, a professor of urban design at Georgia Tech, explains in a 2010 TED Talk based on her book *Retrofitting Suburbia*. In the talk she suggests ideas and strategies for "urbanizing" abandoned or declining suburban malls, shopping centers, and big box stores. This involves updat-

---

2. Oro Valley Main Streets Project, accessed August 1, 2016, https://www.oro valleyaz.gov/mainstreets.

ing these types of developments with higher density mixed-use (residential/office/retail) projects that are walkable, bikeable, and more accessible by public transit. For Dunham-Jones, retrofitting the suburbs is a creative way to combat sprawl, build more sustainable communities, increase neighborliness, and form more interesting communities that were once defined primarily by their blandness.

What if we applied this retrofitting concept to the church, both literally and figuratively? In a literal sense churches can retrofit by rethinking how their physical space functions in a neighborhood. What would it mean for your church to be a true third place or "mixed-use" development that is a vital resource in the neighborhood? What could your church look like as community center, park, preschool, coffee shop, and affordable housing development? Whether it's one or all of them, what does it look like not just to have these things as programs and extra revenue streams but to see them as adding to the fabric of the community and the furthering of God's kingdom? Beyond the brick and mortar we also need to apply the lessons we're learning from the urban core about culture-making, building community, and finding spiritual connection and transformation to churches both urban and suburban.

I believe the church needs to do some deep soul searching. The Coronado Neighborhood and others may have a high sense of neighborliness because they have great "soul." In their paper "Rituals: emotions, community faith in soul and the messiness of life," Hustedde and King suggest that communities and neighborhoods often develop their own soul. In communities where there is a deep sense of emotion, soul, and spirit, members of the community find meaning and their "authentic self."[3] Many of our churches have lost their soul and their authentic self, and they're just going through the motions to keep the lights on and a full-time pastor in the pulpit. Other churches have become insular and exclusive out of fear for their neighbors, both the ones who physically surround them and anyone else they feel is different from them and who threatens their values.

As we discern how the church may undergo a similar fundamental shift as our cities have, we should be cognizant of the warning that Ellen-Dunham and June Williamson provide when speaking of retrofitting the suburbs:

> Some of the changes will be incremental—a change of use here, a new street or building there, much as one sees in the "incremental urbanism" that characterizes the perception of how the world's great cities evolved over time. However, American suburban development patterns are so highly specialized for single uses that their layouts are resistant to incremental adaptation. Consequently, the most effective redevelopments will be those that retrofit the streets, blocks, and lots to provide a compact, connected, walkable mix of uses and housing types. Unfortunately, projects at this scale often evoke criticism as "instant cities" or "faux urbanism." The challenge for all involved is to provide settings and buildings that transcend their "instant" status and inspire their communities.[4]

---

3. Ronald Hustedde and Betty King, "Rituals: emotions, community faith in soul and the messiness of life," *Community Development Journal* 37 (4): 338–48.

4. Ellen Dunham-Jones and June Williamson, "Retrofitting Suburbia," *Urban Land*, June 2009, http://uli.org/wp-content/uploads/2009/10/Sustainable-Suburbs -Retrofitting-Suburbia.pdf.

It could be easy to take the examples we've shared throughout the book and simply reproduce them in your own context, but in many cases that would be unwise. Starting a Theology Pub concept or opening a coffee shop for the sake of "reaching new people" would be to miss the point. Instead, and to reiterate a point from an earlier chapter, start with talking to your neighbors. Start spending time at the neighborhood bar, local coffee shop, farmer's market, art gallery, and other spaces where community is happening. Observe, but also participate. Meet people and get to know them, seeking to understand them. Collaborate with your neighbors. Partner with other faith communities, nonprofits, businesses, entrepreneurs, and governments to make your community a better place. Be part of creating a rich, deep, and interesting fabric in your neighborhood. Be a part of the work God is always doing to increase beauty, what is interesting, what is compelling, what is compassionate, and what is loving. There are no instant strategies or magic pills here, only intentional discernment of God's call and the willingness to recognize and participate in the ways that God is working outside of our comfort zones.

This will be challenging and even scary for some. It's scary because the model of a building with a professional pastor is all we've ever known. Yet this model has turned us not into disciples but into consumers. We've become overly dependent on the business model of corporate and franchised church. We need to be reminded that Jesus called us to lives of selflessness and abundance, not lives of consumerism and scarcity.

The sixth chapter of John's Gospel begins with the narrative of Jesus feeding five thousand hungry people who were following him. He takes five loaves of bread and two fish, the only food available to him, and miraculously feeds the multitude of people. The text then says, "When the people saw the sign that he had done, they began to say, 'This is indeed the prophet who is to come into the world.' When Jesus realized that they were about to come and take him by force to make him king, he withdrew again to the mountain by himself" (John 6:14-15 NRSV). This is a curious passage. Didn't Jesus want to be king? Wasn't the whole point that God had come to earth to defeat God's enemies and rule forever? This is the Jesus that many worship, the Jesus who sits at the right hand of God as military ruler. This is the Jesus that takes care of his own, promising power, status, and prosperity to his most loyal followers. So why does Jesus escape his own coronation ceremony? Because he wasn't interested in being the kind of king that the crowd wanted or hoped he'd be. Yes, he would eventually be crowned "king," mockingly as "King of the Jews" as he was beaten and then tortured to death by the Roman authorities. The king Jesus would become was a king who would die, not just for his people but for all people. He would die to expose the power of death, violence, fear, hate, and oppression. He would die as one who fed the hungry, healed the sick, loved the marginalized and outcast, and liberated the oppressed. His resurrection showed that his death was not in vain and that life, love, forgiveness, and inclusion will always triumph over the darkness.

Have we lost sight of the Jesus we are called to follow? Are we instead chasing a Jesus who we think will give us bigger, better, more comfortable lives and defend us from our enemies? The Jesus who calls us to love God and love our neighbor is at work, whether we are following him or not. He's at work when neighbors care for one another. He's at work when friends gather at the neighborhood bar. He's at work in the interfaith dinner and dialogue between different religious groups. He's at work in the yoga class and on the hiking trail. He's at work in urban churches and suburban churches. He's at work at potlucks, even church potlucks. It's up to us whether or not we choose to recognize where Jesus is at work and then decide if we will follow him in moving that work forward.

(Dottie) So now we have some work to do. We have the work of release: to release what have been our sacred cows and our understanding of the church. And we have the work of search and find: searching for the places where God is working and finding the new way that is connecting today's populations with God. Most of what Rob and I have talked about is structural change. We resist it; however, it is easier to change our structure than our heart.

We didn't know how we would end this book. We left that open to the discovery process. But the things we have seen as we opened our eyes to a new way have been both understandable and astonishing. We can imagine the new way of being church, but the harder work is in imagining the transformation process. God will lead us there if we are willing to jump off a few cliffs, travel in the dark woods, and look for the ocean and the chapel. God has promised that the church will live on, but God did not promise that it will live on in the way that brings us comfort.

My niece and I have been having a conversation. She doesn't go to church. She is deeply spiritual but not religious. I am spiritual and religious. We have been bantering back and forth about whether the church has any place in culture. She agrees that we provide a touchpoint of community connection that is needed. But her critique is around the word worship and around the hypocrisy she sees and the way the idea of "forgiveness" seems to give an easy pass to those who have committed great sins. And she is critical of the abuses of power that seem to reside in the church. But she wants us to be better. She hopes that we can bring some source of betterment to society and that our hope for the world will not die out. And that is where we agree. I want us to be better and to be a source of hope for the world that is facing great transformation with fear and trepidation. I'm thinking that the "rocks crying out" is a good thing. I'm thinking we will learn from the "rocks." We are thinking that God is using the movement in the world to change the church.

And so, Rob and I agree, there is something sacred about the secular.